The Victory of the Cross

By Erskine White

D0067520

C.S.S. Publishing Company, Inc.
Lima, Ohio

THE VICTORY OF THE CROSS

Copyright © 1991 by
The C.S.S. Publishing Company, Inc.
Lima, Ohio

Library of Congress Cataloging-in-Publication Data

White, Erskine, 1951-
    Victory of the cross / by Erskine White.
       p.   cm.
    Includes index.
    ISBN 1-55673-227-5
    1. Lenten sermons. 2. Easter—Sermons. 3. Sermons, American.
4. United Church of Christ—Sermons. 5. Reformed Church—Sermons.
6. United churches—Sermons. 7. Children's sermons. I. Title.
BV4277.²55 1991
252'.62—dc20   90-44131
                                               CIP

9110 / ISBN 1-55673-277-5

DEDICATION

dedicated to the memory of

Frank Putnam White
1929-1979
a prophet to the churches

*"But the souls of the righteous
are in the hand of God . . .
Having been disciplined a little
they will receive great good."*

— Wisdom of Solomon 3:1, 5

Table of Contents

A Word About Language

The language in this book pertaining to people is inclusive of men and women. Similarly, the anecdotes and illustrations have been deliberately varied so as to include the experiences of women and men alike. As for the language pertaining to God, I have used pronouns (generally, "He" for God and "She" for the Holy Spirit). It is necessary to use pronouns in order to preserve the Biblical view that ours is a personal God. Whenever it appears, however, the pronoun is always initiated by a capital "H" (or "S"), indicating to the reader that God is neither male nor female in human terms.

E. White

Introduction

The *Star Spangled Banner* is performed at thousands of American sporting events every year, and those who perform it are continually faced with the challenge of bringing fresh interpretations to familiar material. For its part, the audience appreciates the difficulty and responds more warmly than usual when someone offers an innovative treatment of the oft-sung anthem.

The Christian preacher or speaker faces the same dilemma in preparing for Lent. After all, the Passion story and its attendant texts don't change, so after years of working with them, even the most enthusiastic and experienced pastor can begin to wonder how often he or she can sing the same songs in new and different ways.

Similarly, the dedicated laypersons seeking Lenten devotions and inspiration can also find it difficult to approach the texts and themes of the season with fresh and faithful eyes. In short, Lent offers rich spiritual opportunities to the preacher and practicing Christian, but it also poses the problem of how to put new wine in old and well-used wineskins.

The sermons, prayers and children's lessons which follow are meant to offer some assistance to Christian clergy and laity alike in this regard. Thus, there is a variety of sermon subjects in these pages, as well as a variety of sermon styles — expository, pastoral, prophetic, a story sermon, even a sermon which is ten "mini-sermons" in one! Hopefully, readers will find in this diversity some new ideas, approaches or anecdotes which will help them in their own creative work during this important time of the Christian year.

Throughout the Bible, there are dialectics between evil and good, sin and grace, worldliness and freedom, judgment and good news. Nowhere is this more apparent or important than during Lent. Lent is a season for repentance, solemnity, sacrifice and Crucifixion. It is also a season for hope, joy, renewal and Resurrection. The sermons in this book seek to present these two poles of Lenten spirituality in Biblical balance, without letting one outweigh the other.

If we ignore or minimize the power of sin in our lives or in the world, we trivialize the agony of the cross. On the other hand, if we minimize the power and promise of redemption, we dismiss the victory of the cross. Neglecting the former makes religion naive and superficial; neglecting the latter renders it helpless and morose. Needless to say, the good news of Jesus Christ isn't meant to do either.

As many preachers are fond of saying, we have an Easter faith, but we live in a Good Friday world. During Lent, we should remain committed to expressing both these realities. We should be willing to enter the depths — even "the valley of the shadow" — but never lose sight of the amazing grace and incomparable glory which are yet to come.

— *Rev. Erskine White*
Melrose, Massachusetts

Dust And Ashes
Text: Genesis 18:22-33

Behold, I have taken upon myself to speak to the Lord,
I who am but dust and ashes.   (Genesis 18:27)

Tonight begins the forty-day season of Lent: forty days which correspond to the time Jesus spent in the desert wilderness being tempted by Satan. It is not a season we should enter into unadvisedly or lightly, for this is the most important part of the Christian year. Here we encounter our faith in all its fullness: in all its depth and height, in all its darkness and light, in all its pain and glory.

Lent is a somber time, a time for reflection and growth, a time to change our ways and deepen our commitment. Our Lord entered into suffering and death during this period on our behalf. The least we can do is enter into the spiritual demands of the season for Him.

This Lenten season will carry us through the next five Sundays. We will walk in the shadow of the Cross. We will taste the dryness of the desert and feel the loneliness of the wilderness. If we truly step into the spirituality of the Lenten season, we will feel like we have walked through the valley and shadow of death itself.

Then we will come to Holy Week. We will see the triumph and tension of Palm Sunday, when Jesus rode into Jerusalem and set the stage for His final passion. We will see the trial and tribulation of Maundy Thursday, when Jesus was arrested and condemned to death. We will stare into the unspeakable darkness of Good Friday, when our Lord hung on a Cross to die.

And then, finally, we will come to the bright light and magnificent redemption of Easter morning. The Resurrection will

11

be real and meaningful to us because we will have walked to Calvary to get there. Again, if we really enter into the spirit of Lent in the forty days ahead, we will be happy and grateful for our Lord's victory when it finally comes on Easter Sunday.

But tonight we begin with dust and ashes. Tonight we begin by hearing Abraham speak for all of us: "Behold, I have taken upon myself to speak to the Lord, I who am but dust and ashes."

Who among us would care to say this about ourselves? How many of us can be as honest as Abraham? It goes against the grain, doesn't it, this spirituality of dust and ashes.

It stands in contrast to the superficial piety and self-seeking silliness which too often passes for religion today. It contradicts the religion of self-esteem; it violates the "Praise the Lord and give me the goodies" religion which this self-satisfied age is content to hear. But scripture says that to everything, there is a season. There is a time to "make a joyful noise unto the Lord," and there is a time for dust and ashes.

Tonight is Ash Wednesday. It is a time to strip away our vanities and delusions. It is a time for dust and ashes.

"Behold I have taken upon myself to speak to the Lord, I who am but dust and ashes." It may not sound so at first, but this spirituality of dust and ashes is good and healthy for us. It leads us to admit our frailty and confess our sin.

Of course, we're not surprising God or telling Him anything new, since God already knows our sin; but we are telling ourselves, and that is good. It is no accident Jesus began His Sermon on the Mount by saying, "Blessed are the poor in spirit . . . (Blessed are those who know their need for God)" (Matthew 5:3).

The Bible teaches that spiritual pride is the most fundamental of all sins, because it keeps us from knowing our need for God. But Abraham knew. He stood before God and said, "I am but dust and ashes." The great King David confessed, "For I know my transgressions, and my sin is everywhere before me" (Psalm 51:3). The apostle Paul, one of history's most towering Christians, cried out, "Wretched man that I am!" (Romans 7:24).

In marked contrast, the spirit of this present age wants to say, "I'm okay and you're okay." But which is the more honest, more spiritual assessment of who we are in this fallen world?

Yes, the spirituality we find in scripture requires honesty in oneself. In fact, the first letter of John says it with unavoidable clarity: "If we say we have no sin, we deceive ourselves, and the truth is not in us" (1:8).

But our confession of sin also means that we respect the integrity of God. If we are at all impressed with the majesty and holiness of God, then we must also be impressed with our own lowliness, and with how far we fall short of His glory.

The timeless confessions of Abraham and David and Paul are so great and powerful precisely because they hold God in awe, and this is what so many Christians miss today. When we fail to grasp the depths of our sin, we fail to grasp the glory of God, and our faith is all the poorer for it.

We begin with dust and ashes tonight, but it is important to know that we do not end there. Finally, it is the goodness and mercy of God we dwell on, not just our own unworthiness.

We see this in our text this evening. Abraham makes his magnificent confession as he bargains with God, but the whole story is about God's mercy! If there are fifty righteous people in Sodom, God will spare the city. For the sake of forty-five and then forty good people, He won't destroy the city.

Finally, for the sake of ten, God says, "If, in the whole city of Sodom there are but ten righteous people, I will spare the city." Most people focus this story on Sodom's sin or Abraham's plea. What they miss is God's mercy! God is bending over backwards to be merciful to the sinful human community.

We are worshiping in that spirit tonight. We began by confessing our sins, but we end here at the table, the place of our redemption and reconciliation with God.

So tonight, I invite you to be like Abraham in this Lenten season, and tell God who you are. Tell God boldly, even joyfully, for confession starts the path to redemption. Let us all make bold to speak to the Lord from the depths of our hearts, we who are but dust and ashes. The amazing thing is: God loves us still and is always there to listen. Amen.

Pastoral Prayer

Almighty God, who judges all the earth and everyone in it, and who knows our sin better than we can know it ourselves, hear the prayers which we, Your weak and faithless servants, bring before You now:

> For the times we have done wrong even as we knew it was wrong; hear our prayers, O Lord.

> For the times we have spoken the ill-considered word or failed to offer the comforting word when it was needed: hear our prayers, O Lord.

> For the times we have let fear drive out faith and preferred comfort over commitment: hear our prayers, O Lord.

> For our indifference to others in need, our callousness to their pain and our ignorance of their plight; for our easy conscience in a world where millions groan under the burden of poverty and the yoke of injustice: hear our prayers, O Lord.

Most merciful and patient God, who sets before us the bread of life in the midst of our death, forgive us. Accept us at the table tonight. Ease our hunger and quench our thirst with this sacred meal, that we who are but dust and ashes may partake of Your grace and share in Your salvation. We ask all these things, putting our trust not in ourselves, but in our Lord and Savior, Jesus Christ. Amen.

first sunday in lent
The Significance Of An Insignificant Man
Text: Luke 23:18-31

*They seized one Simon of Cyrene . . . and laid on him
the cross, to carry it behind Jesus.*   (Luke 23:26)

We might call Simon of Cyrene a rather insignificant man
in the larger sweep and sway of scripture. He's not a major
figure; in fact, the Bible mentions him just once, almost in
passing: "They seized one Simon of Cyrene, who was coming
in from the country, and laid on him the cross, to carry it behind Jesus."

It is worth noting that Simon was an African, from the
city of Cyrene in what is now northern Libya. He was probably a Jew, since there was a large Jewish community in Cyrene, and he had two sons who later became well-known
Christians (cf. Mark 15:21). That's all we know about him,
a rather insignificant man.

But this insignificant man happened to be in Jerusalem on
the day Jesus was crucified. Against his will, Simon of Cyrene became a part of Jesus' life, and Jesus a part of his. What
do you think Simon saw, and how do you think he felt on that
day of days as he witnessed the most important event in the
history of the world? Come with me now and try to imagine.

Imagine this visitor from Africa making his way through
the narrow, crowded streets of the city. Merchants are hawk-
ing their wares as people scurry by. Children are racing after
one another across the paving stones. There is all the hustle
and bustle one would expect in a great city like Jerusalem.

Suddenly, at the intersection ahead of him, Simon hears
a loud commotion. Some women are crying and wailing in
grief, but other bystanders are cheering. People rush by as
Simon presses up against the wall by the side of the street and
watches.

15

Now he sees the Roman soldiers coming around the corner, heading his way. One soldier carries a banner which flutters in the breeze, another wears a sword which glistens in the sunlight. A third is holding a whip, cursing the crowd and ordering them to stand back. The soldiers are marching someone to his death.

As the procession makes its way toward Simon, he sees a Man with a heavy crossbeam tied to His shoulders. The Man is a gruesome sight. His body is covered with welts and bruises. His hair is matted with blood from a crown of thorns which has been driven into His scalp. People who line the sides of the street are jeering at Him. Every so often, someone breaks out from the crowd to spit in His face. Simon shudders silently. He has never seen such hatred in a crowd of people before.

The Man carrying the cross stumbles and falls and a soldier starts whipping Him: "Get up, You pathetic King of the Jews! Get up and don't make me waste any more of my time on You!"

The man rises slowly to His feet and staggers a few more steps, but then He falls again. Suddenly Simon freezes and time stands still: "You there! You foreigner! Come here and carry this cross!" A Roman soldier is pointing at him! Before Simon can move, he is grabbed by the arm and thrown back to the ground. The soldiers are tying the cross to his back.

Now Simon of Cyrene is closer to this Man than anyone else, and he looks into His eyes. What powerful, penetrating eyes! The kind of eyes that see below the surface right to the soul. The Man's eyes are filled with pain and sorrow, but He seems to feel pity for the people who are putting Him to death.

The Man opens his mouth to speak. "Thank you," He says softly as Simon is pulled to his feet. The Man says nothing to the people who mock and jeer Him but speaks to the women who are shedding their tears for Him:

> Daughters of Jerusalem, do not weep for Me,
> but weep for yourselves, and for your children,
> "For behold, the days are coming when they will say,
> Blessed are the barren, and the wombs that
> never bore, and the breast that never gave suck!"

What a strange thing, Simon thinks, that this Man would say nothing to His enemies and prophesy against His friends.

Maybe Simon was afraid as he was pulled from the crowd. Maybe he was afraid the Romans would crucify him, too, because Romans didn't respect Africans any more than Israelites.

Maybe Simon was angry and resented being made part of another Man's execution. Maybe he felt pity for Jesus and was glad to relieve Him of His burden. Maybe Simon was simply too exhausted to feel anything as he dragged that heavy cross through the streets of Jerusalem and outside the city wall and up the hill to the place of the skull.

We will never know. But someone must have asked him his name and where he was from, because scripture records it for all posterity: Simon of Cyrene carried Jesus' cross to Calvary.

This was an insignificant man who did a very significant thing. He brought Jesus' words to life, for Jesus had said to His disciples, "If any would come after Me, let them deny themselves and take up their cross and follow Me" (Matthew 16:24). And Jesus was also to tell them, "Truly I say to you . . . you will stretch out your hands, and another will gird you and carry you where you do not wish to go" (John 21:18). The very first one to do this — the very first one to pick up a cross and follow Jesus Christ — was an African who happened to be passing by, an ordinary man named Simon of Cyrene.

You and I are rather ordinary people like Simon, so perhaps we can see ourselves in his place today. Perhaps there is an important lesson in his story for the living of our own lives.

It's true, isn't it, that the burdens we carry in life are often thrust upon us involuntarily. Like Simon of Cyrene, we are passing by through the days of our lives when suddenly, we are seized against our will and given a cross to bear.

It happens so often that it's hard to know where to begin listing the examples of the "Simon situations" in life.

A young child or a young adult is suddenly struck by a fatal, incurable disease. Now, at a too-young age, he must come to terms with life and death, and he must learn courage in the living of whatever time he has left. Maybe you've heard of the seven-year-old boy who got AIDS through the transfusion of tainted blood. What a cross to bear! He didn't ask for that — no AIDS victim does — it was thrust upon him against his will. What a cross to bear.

A young mother is left alone to raise children that the father can't be bothered with. She didn't ask for this abandonment and abuse; it was thrust upon her against her will. Now she must struggle to be both a breadwinner and a mother. That is her cross to bear.

A father is unemployed, or forced to take a lower wage job, because the company wants higher profits and cheaper labor overseas. Now he must find a way to keep his self-respect and keep his family fed. He didn't ask for this hardship. He is not responsible for the callousness of mammon's market-place. It was thrust upon him against his will, and this is his cross to bear.

Finally, I can't even begin to count all the families which patiently struggle with the failing health of their elder loved ones. Children care for aging parents; husbands and wives help an ailing spouse. No one asks to be in such situations, but this is a cross most of us bear in one way or another.

It seems we receive most of our burdens in life the way Simon of Cyrene received his — unexpectedly and against our will. This is a fact of life we cannot change. But we can decide how we will respond to our burdens. We can grow bitter and curse God or the fates for thrusting these injustices upon us, or we can accept our crosses as part of the fabric of life, and find through Christ the strength to carry on. One is a defeat while the other is a victory over the circumstances of life.

Earlier, when I was telling you Simon's story, you remember how I said that when Simon picked up Jesus' cross, he was closer to our Lord than anyone else on earth. Simon was just inches away from the Master's face when they threw him down and tied the cross to his back, and when he followed Christ to Calvary.

This is the secret to all the "Simon situations" we face in life. We must know that like Simon, we are truly closest to Jesus when we bend down and pick up the cross which lies before us. We are most like Christ when we sacrifice for someone else, when we bear each other's burdens with dignity and grace.

This is how He turns our burdens into blessings, He who has "surely borne our griefs and carried our sorrows" (Isaiah 53:4). He allows us to join Him in our afflictions. Pick up your cross in life and bear it willingly, and you will find that Christ is more real to you than ever before, and you are more alive in Him.

If you are looking for the path to new life in Jesus Christ this Lenten season, you won't find it with the "Christian industries" today — with the big business Christian broadcasters and religious trinket-makers. You won't find it in the way they market our Lord for profit. You see, they probably won't tell you about things like denying yourself and picking up a cross because that is bad for ratings and profits. They fear they won't survive unless they offer what the public will buy and wants to hear.

Instead, look for the truth you seek in Jesus Christ, and in Jesus Christ alone. He has already told us and shown us all we need to know. His words and deeds are plain and true.

Lose your life in order to gain it. Give to others and don't worry about receiving. Don't gain the world and lose your soul. Love your enemies, and pray for those who hurt you.

Don't live for this world or the things of this world, but seek first the Kingdom of God. Seek greatness by being a servant. Most of all, if you would live with Jesus Christ today — if you want Him to be real and Lord of your life — deny yourself and pick up your cross, and follow Him to Calvary.

Simon of Cyrene came along to show us explicitly what Jesus was talking about. Simon was just an ordinary person like you or me, but remember his story today, and make it your own.

God was watching as this insignificant man did something eternally significant, as he picked up the cross of Jesus Christ. And Simon of Cyrene lives even now to hear Jesus thank him in heaven. Amen.

Pastoral Prayer

Most Holy and Faithful God, whose Son, Jesus, is bearing His cross for us even today, we pray for courage, humor and grace in meeting the trials and tribulations of life. Help us not to complain too much, or impose our sorrows on others. Help us to save tomorrow's troubles for tomorrow, so we may live better and more cheerfully today.

Most of all, dear God, help us to see our Savior beside us when we stumble and fall. Help us to lose ourselves in Him when we have our crosses to bear, that He might give us renewed hope and strength for the living of these days.

Finally, Most Righteous and Loving Lord, we pray that as we walk along the highways and byways of life, we will be moved by Your Spirit to help bear the burdens of others in need. Move us quickly to aid the aged and infirm, the poor and oppressed, the lonely and discouraged. Lead us to help, and like Simon of Cyrene, even to pick up their cross from the blood-soaked street and carry it up the hill to Calvary. O Precious Lord and Savior, don't leave us too timid or afraid to heal the wounds around us. You have carried our cross and borne our burdens. Now help us to do the same for others. Through Jesus Christ, our Lord. Amen.

children's lesson
Going Along With The Crowd
Text: Luke 23:18-31

But they all cried out together . . . "Crucify Him!"
(Luke 23:18, 21)

When I was a young child, about seven or eight, I knew a boy named _____, and everyone loved to make fun of this guy! They made fun of him because he was big and fat, he was slow and clumsy, he had pimples, and his glasses were always crooked on his face. In other words, there were a lot of reasons to make fun of poor _____. I guess he was the most unpopular kid in school.

One day, I was walking with a group of my friends and we came upon _____. Quick as a flash, everyone surrounded him so he couldn't walk away, and then they started teasing him. They teased him so badly that he started to cry. Mind you, I was there, and I just went along with it. I knew it was cruel and wrong, but I never spoke up to say, "Stop it!" I was afraid that if I did speak up, they would start teasing me.

The Bible says that something very similar happened when Jesus was put to death in Jerusalem. There was a whole crowd of people yelling, "Crucify Him, crucify Him!" Even though Jesus was God's only Son, most of the crowd wanted Him killed. No one dared stand up against the crowd and speak for Jesus' life.

It's hard to stand up against the crowd, isn't it. It's hard to say "no" when all your friends are saying "Yes." It takes courage to be different from the crowd, and sometimes you have to risk being unpopular when you stand up for what is right.

I wish I could tell you it gets easier as you get older, but it doesn't — you'll feel the pressure of the crowd all your life. When you are young, some of your friends might pressure you to disobey your parents or "cut up" in school. They might pressure you to have a drink with them, use drugs, or have sex when you know you shouldn't. When you are older and working in the business world, you might feel pressured to cheat a little bit here, or cut an ethical corner there, because after all, "everybody else is doing it," and you'll never get ahead by "rocking the boat."

So, you might as well decide right now what you are going to do. If you were with a group of friends who were going to do something you knew was wrong, would you say "no" and walk away, or would you "go along with the crowd" and do it anyway? Whenever you are tempted to do what everyone else is doing, try to remember how the crowd of people in Jerusalem cried out against the Lord, and how wrong they were to do such a terrible thing! Do you really want to be like that? Try to remember, because it might help you find the strength to do what you know is right. Amen.

The Ten Commandments For Today
Text: Exodus 20:1-20

And the Lord spoke all these words, saying "I am the Lord your God . . ." (Exodus 20:1-2)

Imagine that your job in life is to get up each morning and prepare an egg for someone else to eat.

There are many different ways to prepare an egg: hard-boiled, soft-boiled, poached, fried, baked, scrambled, benedict, souffled, and so on. Now, if you didn't want to get bored and were willing to take a risk, you could constantly be striving for new ways to prepare an egg. If you wanted to play it safe, and you knew that the person for whom you are cooking loves poached eggs, you could prepare the same poached egg every morning, year in and year out.

Preaching a sermon every week is a bit like that. Over the years, I've offered various styles of sermons on many different kinds of issues, but up until now, I've always had one central theme for each sermon. I've always tried to leave the faithful with one primary message each time.

However, I want to try something different with this sermon. It is about the Ten Commandments, but it isn't just one sermon about them. Instead, I'll give each of the commandments, and then try to fill them out with a little commentary on each one. I will also mention what Jesus said about these commandments, which God first gave to Moses. My purpose is to give you a sense of what each commandment might mean in our modern world.

So, in essence, what follows is ten mini-sermons. You might say that you are getting your eggs scrambled this time, instead of poached, like you usually get them. There is no grand theme, no effort to tie everything together, just ten short, separate sermons on "The Ten Commandments For Today."

• • •

(1) *"I am the Lord your God, who brought you out of the land of Egypt, out of the house of bondage. You shall have no other gods before Me."*

You cannot worship more than one god. You cannot have a first god and a second god, because if you have a second god, your first god isn't really the one true God.

You cannot have more than one god, even if you worship just one at a time. You cannot worship God today, and then set Him aside for a few hours tomorrow because He interferes with your lifestyle, your ambitions or your business. It is all or nothing. You worship one God all the time, or you worship no god at all.

Jesus said that "No one can serve two masters, for you must end up hating one and loving the other . . . You cannot serve God and mammon" (Matthew 6:24). God alone must have the first claim upon your mind and the first loyalty of your heart, more than money, more than family or nation, more than anything or anyone else in this world. "You shall have no other gods before Me."

(2) *"You shall not make yourself a graven image or any likeness . . . you shall not bow down to them or serve them . . ."*

You shall not make an idol or icon to worship. You shall not pray to any statue or saint or image whatsoever; nor shall you pray to a Christian symbol such as a medallion, as if it were a lucky charm.

You shall not portray God in any human likeness, male or female. Nor shall you look at a beautiful sunset or a stirring scene from nature as if this were a picture of God. God cannot be contained in nature, any more than He can be captured in an image or portrait made with human hands. The appearance of the God who made heaven and earth is beyond our imaginings.

You shall not make other idols and serve them, putting them above the Lord your God. You shall not make an idol of your possessions or your standard of living, your nation or race. You shall not idolize a preacher, a politician or your favorite entertainer, who are made of flesh and blood. You shall not make an idol of "the good old days," so that the ways of the past are more important to you than God's will for the future.

Do not make idols of guns and missiles, or trust in them for the security you should find in God. Do not make an idol of your economic system, so as to justify the oppression of the poor by your so-called "laws" of the marketplace. Do not make an idol of any ideology or institution — any power or principality — because all authority is subject to God. "You shall not make yourself any idol or image . . . you shall not bow down to them and serve them."

(3) *"You shall not take the name of the Lord your God in vain."*

The Lord's name is holy, so do not disgrace it by swearing or obscenity. With practice and self-discipline, you can learn to express your anger without profaning the name of the Lord.

Nor shall you repeat the Lord's name or phrases like "thank you Jesus" over and over again in your worship, as if to cast a magic spell of fervor and emotion. The Lord's name is holy and is not for show or entertainment, even from the pulpit.

You shall not use the Lord's name in the service of a political campaign, a business venture, or one nation's cause against another. You shall not justify your pursuit of power, profit or privilege by claiming that "God is on our side."

Jesus told us not to "heap up empty phrases" when we pray or worship, and when He spoke of God in the Lord's Prayer, He said, "Hallowed be Thy name" (Matthew 6:7, 9). God's name is sacred! "You shall not take the name of the Lord your God in vain."

(4) *"Remember the Sabbath day, to keep it holy."*

You shall come to God's house for worship on the Sabbath. God has given you all the world and all the days of the week — you shall give Him the Sabbath day in return.

25

To keep the Sabbath is to confess that the world belongs to God and not to us. From fast food chains to football games, when businesses make employees work on the Sabbath, they are saying that the claims of commerce matter more than the claims of God.

Jesus said that the Sabbath was made for people, not people for the Sabbath (Mark 2:27). This means the Sabbath is meant to help us as a day of rest, not burden us with rigid rules which defy common sense. For example, some businesses and services must certainly remain open on Sunday to cover emergency needs. Also, if the mother in the family must cook or clean on the Sabbath, the father and children should help her with this work, so that she may have a day of rest as well. "Remember the Sabbath day, to keep it holy."

(5) *"Honor your father and your mother, that your days may be long in the land which the Lord your God gives you."*

You shall respect the integrity of the family. Your parents cared for you when you were young, and you shall care for them when they are old. Whether they live in an institution or at home, you owe a debt to your parents which someday your children shall pay to you.

Jesus said that we should do more than honor members of our own household, because we are also part of a larger family. He said that whoever does the will of God is sister and brother, mother and father to Him (Matthew 12:50).

The family is the foundation and the basic unit of society. When the family is respected and parents are honored, the reward is a stable society: "Your days shall be long in the land." And when all people are respected as members of one human family, the whole world is blessed. "Honor your father and your mother."

(6) *"You shall not kill."*

You shall not deprive persons of their most precious right of all: the right to life. You shall not do it on a mass scale, as in war or genocide; nor shall you do it on a small scale, as in one person's violence against another.

You shall not kill people because they are helpless or inconvenient, useless or unprofitable. You shall not kill the aged simply because they are old; allowing someone to die with dignity is far different from so-called "mercy killing." You shall not kill the ignorant or the handicapped. You shall not kill the unborn child, unless certain extenuating circumstances require it. You shall not kill the hungry and homeless by ignoring their cries for food and shelter. You shall respect the sanctity of life, from the womb to the tomb, because life is a gift from God.

Jesus said even more than this. He said that you shall not even be angry or hateful toward others (Matthew 5:22), since spiritual violence and physical violence are different only in kind, not in degree. You shall not threaten others, either with a gun in your hand or a nuclear missile in your silo. You shall not promote hatred of your enemy with talk of "evil empires" when you are also evil yourselves. You must learn the message of Jesus: that love is the only way to overcome an enemy, and justice is the only path to peace. "You shall not kill."

(7) *"You shall not commit adultery."*

You shall respect the institution of marriage and remain faithful to your wedding vows. You shall not succumb to a hedonistic culture which preaches pleasure over principle and confuses liberty with license. Marriage is more than a merger of bodies; it is also the deeper union of souls. Sometimes there is a need for divorce in a failed or brutal marriage, but there is never an excuse for infidelity along the way.

Again, Jesus takes this still further by saying that you shall not even lust after someone other than your spouse, for then you have committed adultery in your heart (Matthew 5:28). To commit adultery in a bed or simply in your heart is, again, a difference without a distinction.

You shall not commit adultery by other means as well. You shall not become "married" to your job, or neglect your spouse for excessive outside interests or ambitions. If you abandon your spouse like this, how is it different than if you took on a lover? God has been faithful to you, so you should be faithful to one another. "You shall not commit adultery."

27

(8) *"You shall not steal."*

You shall not take what isn't yours. Stealing from a large, faceless institution is no better than mugging a poor widow on the street. Even when no one is looking, you shall not steal.

You also shall not steal in more sophisticated ways, even when they are legal. You shall not steal by charging excessive prices for your goods or services, or by paying your workers less than a living wage. You shall not steal from your children by polluting the earth for your own short-term profit. You shall not steal by enriching yourself at the expense of the poor.

Jesus said that instead of being concerned with hoarding our possessions, we should be giving them away (Matthew 5:42). If someone asks you for a coat, give her two. Lay up treasure for yourself in heaven, not on earth, remembering that it is more blessed to give than to receive. "You shall not steal."

(9) *"You shall not bear false witness against your neighbor."*

You shall be honest in all your dealings, and tell the truth. You shall not accuse your neighbor falsely — whether that neighbor is someone down the street or a hostile nation halfway around the world. Even when it is to your advantage to tell a lie or just part of the truth, be kind and trustworthy in your speech.

Jesus didn't stop by saying that we shouldn't swear falsely; He said we shouldn't swear at all. Don't swear by heaven, for that is the throne of God; and don't swear by earth, for that is God's footstool (Matthew 5:34). Just tell the truth with a "yes" or "no" — don't swear by anything that you are doing it. "You shall not bear false witness against your neighbor."

(10) *"You shall not covet your neighbor's house . . . or anything else that is your neighbor's."*

Do not set your heart on things your neighbors have. Do not let conspicuous consumption or the culture of corporate advertising make you hunger and thirst for material things. Do not be obsessed with "keeping up with the Joneses," for the Joneses have already received their reward.

Jesus taught that instead of coveting the things of this world, we should covet the things of God. Covet God's love, and the love of one another. Covet the fruits of faith, joy and peace. Do not be consumed by things that rust and rot away, but live for things eternal. "Blessed are those who [covet] righteousness," Jesus said, "for they shall be satisfied" (Matthew 5:6). "You shall not covet . . . anything that is your neighbor's."

• • •

Those are "The Ten Commandments For Today." If you feel guilty or convicted by one or more of these commandments, I have just one thing to say to you: welcome to the human race! I myself felt guilty as I wrote some of these words. Welcome to the human race, and welcome to the good feeling of knowing why Jesus calls you especially blessed today: "Blessed are the poor in spirit [who know their need for God], for theirs is the kingdom of heaven" (Matthew 5:3).

If you heard this sermon carefully, you will surely agree that as people and as a nation, we all fall short of these commandments. As people and as a nation, we would do far better to repent and change our ways, which is God's message to us during this season of Lent.

May God help us by writing these commandments upon our hearts, that we may receive the grace of forgiveness and live more fully as children of His kingdom, a kingdom which begins in Jesus Christ, a kingdom which has no end. Amen.

Pastoral Prayer

O Holy and Righteous God, who gave the law to Moses that we may live well with one another according to Your ways, come to us now and write Your law upon our hearts. Open our hearts and minds to Jesus, and let His love rise up deep within us, that we may live the law not by duty but by grace. Teach us to be free of the law

in order that we may fulfill the law . . . that we may live all our days with one God, one Lord, with righteousness and peace towards all Your children. In Jesus' name we pray. Amen.

Bibliography: *Interpreter's Bible,* Vol. I, (Abingdon Press, Nashville, 1952), pp. 979-989.

The Consequences Of Sin
Text: Exodus 20:1-20

For I the Lord your God am a jealous God, punishing children for the iniquity of parents to the third and the fourth generation of those who hate Me . . .

(Exodus 20:5b)

If your brother, your sister, or even a friend of yours does something bad, do you think you should be punished for it? Should you be punished for something your parents did wrong many years ago, or even your grandparents and great-grandparents?

It doesn't seem fair, does it. I mean: you get in enough trouble all by yourself, without getting into trouble for someone else! But in one of the Ten Commandments, it says that this is just what happens. If a father or mother does something evil, their children, their grandchildren and even their great-grandchildren will have to pay for it.

Jesus came along more than a thousand years after this law was given, and He changed the situation (cf. John 9:1-7). He showed us how God would rather heal us of our sin than punish us for it. But there is still an important message here just the same — the message is that we don't just hurt ourselves when we commit sin, and our sin isn't over the minute we stop it. Sin has consequences which can touch far more people and last much longer than we realize.

Think about the boy or girl who cheats in school. Week in and week out, on tests and quizzes, this student cheats every chance she gets. Do you think no one else is affected by that? Suppose you were in her class. Suppose you studied hard for a big test and took it honestly, but she got the same grade as you because she cheated. Would that be fair to you? Her sin doesn't just affect her, does it? It affects the whole class, including you!

And the consequences of her sin won't end when the test is over. Because she started off cheating and didn't learn the material, she'll have to keep on cheating just to keep up. Eventually, she will get caught, or she will finish school totally unprepared for the world because she didn't learn anything along the way. Either way, she'll find that the whole rest of her life will be affected by the cheating she had started to do so many years earlier.

Be careful about sin — it can be visited upon even the third and fourth generation. That's the Bible's way of saying that the sin we commit doesn't just affect us; it affects many other people as well. And the consequences of the wrong we do can last far longer than we realize when we first do it. That's the way sin is, and understanding sin like this makes it even more important that we do what is good and right. Amen.

The Boy Who Ran Away
Text: Mark 14:43-52

A young man followed Him, with nothing but a linen cloth about his body; and they seized him, but he left the linen cloth and ran away naked. (Mark 14:51-52)

To understand what follows, cast loose your imagination for the moment. In this sermon, I am going to pretend that I am a Bible character who lived two thousand years ago, and I am writing a letter to the modern-day Christian church. The letter begins as follows:

I.

My name is John Mark. I was a witness to the last night Jesus spent on earth, and I represent all children at the events you call the Passion. Yes, it's true. It wasn't just grown-ups who were with Jesus that final night. I was there, too. I am the boy who ran away naked when they arrested our Lord.

The events I'll describe began with the Last Supper. Do you remember how when Jesus came to Jerusalem, He told His disciples to find a man carrying a jar of water, and how this man took them to a house where they could meet for Passover? Well, I can tell you now that this was a secret signal Jesus used. You see, men didn't carry water; that was a job for women or donkeys. So, when the disciples saw this man, they knew he was a friend who would lead them to a "safe house." Jesus had to use secret signals like this because Jerusalem was full of spies and informers.

You might speculate from the Book of Acts (12:12) that when the man with the water met the disciples, the place he took them to was my mother's house. That's how I came to be there, and how I came to be a witness to the story I am about to tell you.

My mother called me home that afternoon and told me to spend the rest of the day inside. She said that Jesus was coming over soon with some of His friends, and no one could know He was coming. It was dangerous, she said, because there were soldiers in the streets looking to arrest Him. She told me to be quiet about it, and to help her get ready for the Passover meal.

My mother was a brave woman who took a big chance hiding this Man, Jesus. I didn't understand why He was so important or why they wanted to arrest Him, but I did what I was told.

Just as it was getting dark, there was a knock on our door. It was a secret knock the disciples often used, so I knew it was them and opened the door right away. They came in quickly — Jesus and the twelve — and I closed the door behind them.

I led them upstairs to the Upper Room and then went to the kitchen. My mother brought them the Passover bread, and I carried the wine. Then I sat down on the floor in a corner of the room, hoping my mother would let me stay.

I remember that this particular Passover meal was even more solemn than usual, and Jesus seemed especially troubled that night. He spoke softly, but I could hear every word. He told the disciples that He was going to leave them and go to His Father's house in heaven. He said that the world would hate them because of Him. He washed their feet and told them to be servants to others as He was a servant to them (cf. John 13-17).

Jesus spoke for a long time, carefully and earnestly. He was like a teacher before a final exam — it was as if He wanted to teach them everything He could before it was too late. But I don't think they understood what He was saying. I know I didn't.

Then Jesus said that one of the twelve would betray Him, and everyone in the room got upset. They all started speaking at once: "Is it I, Lord; is it I?" I heard them stoutly swear that they would stand by Jesus to the end. That's when my mother came in — she was bringing up some more bread — she saw me there in the corner and told me to go back downstairs.

A few minutes later, Judas came running down the stairs and bolted out the door. I thought it was odd that he hadn't been more careful before going out into the street, but he looked like a mad man. His face was full of pain and rage. Later that evening, I would find out why he had left in such a hurry.

I was downstairs now, and I couldn't hear what was being said any more. But Peter told me later that Jesus had taken the bread and wine as His body and blood. Peter said it was deeply moving. I am happy to see that the church has preserved the sacred memory of this meal, which you call communion.

Things were pretty quiet for a while, and then I heard them singing. When they came down the stairs, they thanked my mother for all her help, and then went out into the night.

Now, my mother had told me to stay at home, and usually I obey her, but this time I slipped out the front door. I knew from the look in Jesus' eyes and the tension in my house that something big was going to happen, and I didn't want to miss it.

I followed them out of the city and up the Mount of Olives, to a garden called Gethsemane. You can still see it today, and I can even show you the tree I hid behind as I watched and listened during the night. You know, olive trees never die once they are planted, and some of those very same olive trees are still there today — the only living witnesses to Jesus in Gethsemane.

Jesus seemed weary, and even a little impatient with His disciples. I heard Him say that Peter would deny Him three times before the cock crowed in the morning. Now, Peter was a big, strong man — a rough and ready fisherman who didn't seem to be afraid of anything! Why would he do something like that?

Then Jesus took three of His disciples and went to a large, flat rock nearby in the garden. I couldn't hear what He was saying, but I could see by His silhouette in the moonlight that He was praying. He prayed so hard that His sweat became like drops of blood (Luke 22:44), and it made me scared.

What was going on? I knew Jesus had enemies, and I had heard He could be tough on the priests and the moneychangers. But Jesus had always been kind and friendly to me; He especially loved the children. I had never seen Him like this before.

Three times, Jesus came back to His disciples and found them fast asleep. I could hear Him clearly now, because He was really upset. I guess it's hard when your friends disappoint you the one time you ask them for help. I heard Him say, "Can't you stay awake with Me even for one hour? You'd better wake up and pray for yourselves, that you don't enter into temptation, because your spirit is willing but your flesh is weak."

More time passed, and all was quiet. Jesus was sitting off by Himself. I began to wonder what He was waiting for, and what I was doing there. The answer came soon enough.

I saw the soldiers coming before I heard them. I looked down toward the city gate and saw a long line of torchlights bobbing up and down in the night, winding its way up the hill like a luminous, disembodied centipede. They were coming toward Gethsemane.

Soon the sight of the torchlights gave way to the sound of marching footsteps. I heard the swords clanging against the armor, a familiar sound to anyone who lived in Jerusalem. One by one, the disciples woke up, and everyone began shouting. There was mass confusion and panic, but there was nowhere to go because the soldiers had the whole place surrounded.

Judas stepped forward out of the shadows and kissed Jesus on the cheek. Then the soldiers grabbed Jesus, and I knew why Judas had run out of my mother's house a few hours earlier. Peter jumped out from the crowd and struck a soldier, but Jesus told him to put away his sword: "Those who live by the sword shall die by the sword." Jesus was true to His convictions to the very end.

I couldn't help but stare at Him. Everyone else had lost their heads. Men were cursing. Soldiers were barking out orders. Only Jesus was calm. He had prayed earlier, remember, and now His strength came from God. It was like He was in control of everything, as if everything was happening according to His plan.

I was watching Jesus when suddenly, a Roman soldier grabbed me. "Here's another one!" he shouted. Instantly, I turned and hit his arm, but when I pulled away from him, he grabbed the linen cloth I was wearing, and my clothes came off in his hands.

As soon as I was free, I ran away — naked as the day I was born! I ran all the way down the hill and through the Kidron and up into the darkened streets of the city. I don't mind telling you I was scared. When I finally got home, my heart was pounding and I started shaking all over. The more I thought about how close I had come to getting arrested with Jesus, the more my body shook uncontrollably. It was a night I shall never forget.

Yes, I was there. I was just a boy who wasn't supposed to leave his mother's house, but I saw it all.

I appear again in the Book of Acts, and in Colossians. I'm mentioned in 2 Timothy, and Philemon, and 1 Peter. It says that my mother's house was the headquarters of the church in Jerusalem. I started to go with Paul on a missionary journey, but then Paul and my cousin, Barnabas, had a terrible argument, and I left with Barnabas. Later, it says that I was reconciled with Paul. I was Paul's assistant, and I was a valuable helper to Peter. They both had good things to say about me in their letters.

Maybe you are wondering: with all I witnessed as a young boy, why would I grow up to join the church? Why would I bother with the church, after seeing how so-called "Christians" act?

As a young boy, I saw one of the disciples sell Jesus' life for thirty pieces of silver. I saw the rest of the disciples deny Him and run away in fear. They were grown men, but they didn't act like it when it counted! For the love of Jesus, at least the women were courageous enough to go to the Cross and be with Him when He died.

Later, I saw Paul arguing with Barnabas. Read between the lines in some of Paul's letters and see how bitterly they spoke to one another. Jesus' followers couldn't even get along among themselves! How could they expect anyone else to believe the gospel of love and peace they preached in His name?

Again I ask: Why would anyone want to be part of the church when they see how Christians behave?

Perhaps you can best answer this question by putting yourselves in our shoes. Suppose, for example you had been with us in Gethsemane. Suppose the Romans had accused you of being a Christian? Would they have had enough evidence to convict you?

It's easy to be critical of what we did. Our shortcomings are right there in the pages of scripture for everyone to see. But I could also be critical of Christians today, for the ways in which you betray our Lord, mistreat one another, and fall asleep when you should be awake. How often has faith faltered and courage failed when the moment of truth has come!

Fortunately, the glory of the church doesn't depend on us. Remember how I stared at Jesus that night in Gethsemane? Christians may be the Body of Christ, but Jesus is the heart and soul of the church. He is the steady one — the salvation you should seek and the light you should follow.

If Christians can be but a dim reflection of His Light, that is enough. Do not judge Christ by Christians, and do not be surprised when Christians fall short of Christ. Remember how the disciples were panicked and confused in the garden, but Jesus was calm and in control.

Remember also, that people can change. Isn't that what this season of Lent is all about? Peter went from coward to martyr. Paul and Barnabas were reconciled. And look at me!

Once, I ran away. I was the boy who ran away. But as I matured, I helped to build up the church. I played my part as best I could. In my case at least, it was not true that the child was father to the man.

My name is John Mark. Some say I wrote the gospel of Mark; some say I didn't. No matter. It's more important that you hear the message of the gospel, rather than argue about who wrote it.

Maybe you've run away when Jesus called you o'er the tumult. Maybe you've fled in fear from the challenge of being faithful. Maybe you've kept the faith when times were easy but failed the test when times got tough.

Well, Christ is still ready to change your life. He is still ready to make you new and strong. I have seen people transformed by the spirit of the Risen Christ. Look what He did for me — the boy who ran away. Amen.

Pastoral Prayer

Gracious and Loving God, we pray for all who must go to dark Gethsemane today — for all who must walk in the valley of the shadows of life. We pray for those who are sick and suffering, and for those who are trapped in the bonds of aimlessness and sin. We pray for those who are alone, without Your Spirit and Presence to keep them company. Most of all, we pray for those who mourn, and for their loved ones who have died. Hear our prayers for everyone who must walk that lonesome valley in these days.

O God, who is our Creator and Sustainer through all the changing circumstances of life, we pray for Your help and guidance when we are weak. Forgive us when we think more of ourselves than our neighbors, when we care more for comfort than commitment. Forgive us when we betray our Lord and reflect badly on His church.

O God, make us new and strong, according to Your Word. Fill us with grace and faith for the living of our days, and make us joyful witnesses to the glory of our Lord. Make us beacons of light to dispel the darkness, and bearers of hope to calm the storm. Through Jesus Christ, we pray for renewal and purpose during this Lenten season. Amen.

children's lesson
Honesty Is The Best Policy
Text: Mark 14:43-52

Day after day I was with you in the temple teaching, and you did not seize Me. (Mark 14:49)

What can we say about the people who arrested Jesus? They did a terrible thing, didn't they. They came with some soldiers and took Jesus away. They put Him in jail and then, the next day, they had Him beaten and killed on a cross. They did this to the Son of God! That is probably the worst thing people have done in the whole history of the world.

But the way they did it is almost as bad as what they did. They arrested Jesus in the middle of the night in a secluded garden outside the city walls; they weren't brave enough to do it in the city or in broad daylight. Jesus noticed this, and He told them He didn't like it. "Look," He said, "I was out there teaching in the temple day after day, in full view of all the people — you could have taken Me there at any time. Where is your courage, that you must come here with soldiers and weapons, sneaking around in the middle of the night?"

Unfortunately, a lot of people are like that today, adults as well as young people. They aren't brave enough to do in the daylight what they will do under the cover of darkness. They act one way to people in public and another way in private. They treat people well to their faces but "do them in" behind their back.

You can really get in trouble by treating people dishonestly like this. For example, have you ever talked badly about someone — like a brother or sister, a friend, a teacher or even your parents — and then turned around to see that person standing there, listening to every word you say? It's worse than embarrassing; it's humiliating! You feel horrible, and you know that no amount of apologizing can erase the words you have said or ease the hurt you have caused.

Even if the person isn't there when you "bad mouth" her behind her back, someone else is sure to tell her what you said, and she won't like it. She'll say to herself, "Why couldn't they tell me to my face, instead of running around under cover of darkness like this, talking behind my back?"

No one likes to be treated like that. You don't like it when someone does it to you! Of course, it's best never to say anything bad about other people. But if a person is doing something you don't like, or treating you in a way you don't like, don't talk about him behind his back. Go and talk to him face to face! Don't complain about someone in secret when you won't do it in the open. Remember that no one trusts a gossip. Remember that when dealing with other people, honesty is usually the best policy. Amen.

Can A Nation Repent?
Text: 2 Chronicles 34:29-33

Then the king gathered . . . all the people great and small; and he read in their hearing all the words of the book . . . (2 Chronicles 34:29-30)

Oftentimes, as we move into the middle of Lent, people begin to grow weary. They begin to ask, "Why all this talk of sin and death? Why must we dwell so long on confession and repentance, "a broken and a contrite heart" (Psalm 51:17)? Who wants to be so gloomy? Let's hear something happy for a change.

Of course, there's no shortage of "happytalk" preachers, and many ministers don't think it's necessary to preach these Lenten themes; but I do, so I think the question deserves an answer.

We dwell on such things for so long because this is the rhythm of the Christian year. "For everything there is a season" (Ecclesiastes 3), so we have Advent to dwell on new birth and new life; we have Pentecost to dwell on the power of the Holy Spirit; and we have the season of Lent to dwell on sin and death.

It is also the rhythm of the Christian's spiritual life. Unless we are honest enough to confess our sin, we won't feel the need to change our ways. And unless we honestly, humbly try to change our ways, there can be no forgiveness. The spiritual life of the mature Christian must always be a rhythm of sin and grace.

Most of us are familiar with Lent as a season to enter into the valley and shadow of personal sin. None of us are the Christians we should be, so it is easy to see why Lent is a time to look into the soul's mirror at our personal shortcomings.

But in the church's hymnbook, there is a hymn which — except for its sexist language — contains a great spiritual truth. It says that in addition to our personal sins, there are also social sins, sins of the nation.

The song was written in the 1840s to protest our war against Mexico. Many Americans at the time felt that this was a sinful war. They felt we were stealing land that didn't belong to us and accused President Polk of deception and aggression.

One young congressman in particular stood up to say, "Allow the President to invade a neighboring country whenever he shall deem it necessary . . . and you allow him to make war at pleasure . . ."

That young, anti-war congressman was named Abraham Lincoln, and the hymn I'm talking about was popular in Lincoln's day. Forgiving, again, it's language, it says,

Once to every man and nation,
comes the moment to decide . . .

A person can sin, and a nation can sin. A person can repent of his or her sin. Can a nation repent? Can a nation change its ways? That is the Lenten question we have before us today.

The Bible is not very hopeful on this score. You may remember how Pharaoh refused to change his ways when confronted with the will of God. Recall how the prophets condemned the sins of the nations — even the sins of Israel — and how the prophets were persecuted for their loyalty to God's Word. Jesus came and wept over the sins of Jerusalem, and in Paul's New Testament letters, we see the church in spiritual combat with the powers and principalities of the world. Finally, in the Book of Revelation, written at a time of terrible trial and struggle with the Roman Empire, the state is called "the beast" (cf. 13:1f, 17:10).

Can a nation repent? Recall the Biblical names and their bloody deeds: Pharaoh, Jezebel, Nebuchadnezzar. Remember Herod, Pilate, and "the beast" of Revelation. Recall how even great kings like David and Solomon committed sin and had to be judged.

Much more often than not, the Bible shows nations to be fountains of iniquity and unrighteousness, at cross-purposes with the ways of God. Surely, God's Word in scripture speaks to people and nations alike: "For My thoughts are not your thoughts, neither are your ways My ways, says the Lord" (Isaiah 55:8).

Many Christians can't accept this. They have distorted Biblical faith to the point where flag is above cross, the dollar is almighty and Caesar is Lord over Christ. They see God in service to nation, instead of nation in service to God. Many Christians today can't believe that God's Word condemns all nations, even their own, but this is the record of scripture.

Even so, there is in the Bible one example of Israel's national repentance, the best example in all of scripture. I refer to the story of King Josiah — which ought to be better known than it is, because this is a story of repentance for all nations in every age.

Josiah became king of Judah in 638 B.C., a period of history not unlike our own. The world was dominated by two superpowers, Assyria and Babylon. There was an arms race, and alliances rose and fell. There were wars and rumors of war; there was terrorism and violence at every turn. The world was in an uproar, and every nation felt that God was on its side.

In the midst of all this turmoil, people sought comfort by looking to the past. There was a feeling in many nations that if people could just get back to the "old time religion," and the values and beliefs of yesterday, the problems of today would go away. (Does that sound familiar to anyone today?)

If you remember the hype and emotion of our own recent program to restore the Statue of Liberty, perhaps you can appreciate how our ancient forebears felt. In Egypt, they set out to restore the pyramids, which were now thousands of years old and in disrepair. In Israel, King Josiah set out to restore the temple, which had also become decrepit. People were fearful and nostalgic. They wanted to return to what they thought were the glory days of old.

45

As they were restoring the temple, the workers came across an old scroll — the Book of the Covenant, which we call Deuteronomy. This was the ancient law which God had given Moses. It had been lost and forgotten for many years, but now it was found. They dusted off the scroll and brought it to the king.

The book was read to the king. It contained the *Shema* of Deuteronomy 6:4 — "You shall love the Lord your God with all your heart, and with all your soul, and with all your mind." It gave rules for worship, and rules for the administration of justice. It also spelled out God's plan of government welfare for the poor, and it said that "there will be no poor among you . . . if only you will obey the voice of the Lord your God" (cf. 15:1f; also Leviticus 25).

As the scroll was read to the king, the words grabbed him at his core. He saw how far his nation had strayed from the ways of God. Our text says he "rent his clothes" — he ripped the clothing he was wearing as a sign of guilt and grief.

Then Josiah did a truly amazing thing, amazing in the sense that it was out of character for a political ruler. He probably had people advising against it, but Josiah assembled all the nation and said, in effect, "I have sinned. We all have sinned, and I've been leading you falsely." Then he held up the scroll: "Here is God's law which we must obey, the commandments we must keep with all our heart and soul if we are to live."

Thus began the greatest reform in Israel's history. Josiah threw out the idols and abominations of Israel; then he moved on to other areas of national life. And God's oracle said to King Josiah: "Because your heart was penitent and you humbled yourself before [Me] when you heard [My] words against this place . . . I also have heard you, says the Lord" (34:27-28).

To be sure, an imperfect world can only repent imperfectly. Jeremiah later thought there was too much emphasis on ritual and not enough on justice and faith. But measured by history, it was an impressive effort. Indeed, the Bible says in 2 Kings that there was no other king like Josiah, before or since (23:25).

What this story tells us is that three things must happen if a nation is to repent of its sins.

First, the wish to repent must spring from God's Word. In Josiah's case, he was humbled by the rediscovery of Deuteronomy. There can be no desire for political gain or economic profit — national repentance must be rooted in God's Word alone.

Next, the act of confession must begin at the top. It must begin with the king, or the president, if you will. The president — any president — must be able to stand before the people and say, "We have all sinned, and I've been leading you in the wrong direction. I know you're used to hearing that God is on our side, but I must tell you today that God is not on our side! God is against us unless we repent and change our ways."

This is what Josiah did. The remarkable thing about him is that as a political ruler, he was still sufficiently humbled by the holiness and majesty of God. Most rulers become too enamored with their own power and prestige; then they are no longer impressed enough with God. But Josiah surely knew in spirit what the prophet was soon to say:

> *Behold, the nations are like a drop from a bucket,*
> *and are accounted as the dust on the scales . . .*
> *[For God] sits above the circle of the earth . . .*
> *[He] brings princes to nought, and makes the*
> *rulers of the earth as nothing.*
> (cf. Isaiah 40:15-23)

When kings (or presidents) truly understand themselves and their God in this way, it shouldn't be too hard for them to confess and repent, even in public when their pollsters and media consultants advise against it.

Repentance must be rooted in God's Word and begin at the top. The third part of national repentance in this story is that it also takes place throughout the whole society. Our text says that all people heard the law, people "great and small"

— business leaders and bureaucrats, soldiers and moneylenders, shepherds and servants, rich, middle class and poor. All people great and small stood before God to say, "I have sinned."

Carried to its fullest, people in business would say, "Forgive us, for we have made an idol of the marketplace." Admirals and generals would say, "Forgive us, for we have made an idol of our weapons." The purveyors of our hedonistic culture would say, "We have made an idol of pleasure." And all people, great and small — every one of us would renounce our own false gods and love the Lord our God with all our heart and soul and mind. National repentance must begin everywhere, even with you and me!

Can a nation repent? Can our nation repent?

We have a slogan printed on our coins: it says, "In God We Trust." We've printed it on our coins since 1864, except for a brief period when President Teddy Roosevelt tried to ban it.

Teddy Roosevelt felt that this slogan was blasphemy, that we cheapen God's name when we use it on our money. He ordered new coins to be minted without the slogan, and guess what happened? All hell broke loose!

The religious lobby — the defenders of national piety — preachers all over America attacked the President. "How dare he remove the Lord from our money! Doesn't he believe in God?"

Fortunately, Congress came to God's rescue, and in a fit of righteous indignation, a law was passed. That's why we still have those four words printed on our money today: "In God We Trust."

Can a nation repent? A nation which cannot say, "Forgive us, Lord, for cheapening Your Name with our love of money," is not a nation ready to repent.

Can a nation repent? More recently, just a few years ago, in fact, Senator Mark Hatfield stood up in the Senate to propose a National Day of Prayer. Now, everyone in Congress loves to vote for national days of prayer, so this resolution passed without opposition. But no one had read what Senator Hatfield's bill actually said.

Hatfield had proposed a National Day of Prayer and Repentance. The bill said, "Forgive us, God, for we have made an idol of our national security." It asked for a day of fasting in America because our nation is six percent of the world's population but uses forty percent of the world's resources. In today's world, filled as it is with deprivation and death, this is just callous greed. The National Day of Prayer Senator Hatfield wanted was a day of national prayer for our sins!

When people begn to read about it, Hatfield's office was flooded with mail. People said, "I'm proud to be an American, and we have nothing to apologize for." People said, "God bless America, and if you don't like it here, why don't you go somewhere else?" They said, "We may have our faults, but we're still the greatest nation on earth."

Can a nation repent? Not when honest criticism is equated with treason. Not when it's good politics to say, "God bless America," and "We're standing tall again," and "The pride is back." My friends, pride is a sin which gets in the way of repentance! A nation which glories in its pride is not a nation ready to say, "God forgive us, for we know not what we do."

Can a nation repent? In the words of the prophets: not when it's good politics, and good business, to "grind the face of the poor" (Isaiah 3:15), and "oppress the fatherless family" (cf. Ezekiel 22:6-7). This is not a nation ready to repent of its selfishness and materialism! This is not a nation ready to hear the Master speak, "Whatsoever you do unto the least of these among you, you do it unto Me" (cf. Matthew 25:31-46).

Jesus often condemned self-righteous people as being the last who will enter the kingdom of heaven. So it is with nations. The nation which is most sure of its righteousness is the nation God loves the least. Is the pride really back? Let's hope not, for pride is something which blocks the path to repentance.

"Once to every man, woman and nation comes the moment to decide." This is the season of Lent. It is time for each of us to ask, "Can I repent?" It is also time to ask, "Can a nation repent?" Remember Josiah, for he showed the way. Amen.

Pastoral Prayer

Almighty God, who is our Guardian in heaven and our Guide as we live on earth, take us on the path to repentance as we travel the road to Calvary this Lenten season. Let us know our guilt, not that we may be paralyzed by remorse or overwhelmed by despair, but that we may then find the real freedom from our guilt which comes from Your forgiveness. Open our eyes to see and our ears to hear, that we may be Your forgiven people from this day forth, and even forevermore.

God of all nations and Lord of history, make our nation repentant as well. Take us away from the politics of pride and the miserable fruits of misplaced patriotism. Make us proud as a nation, not of what we are, but of what we're called to be. Teach us not to glory in our wealth or our might; teach us to glory in the right. Inspire our President, our leaders, and all our people "great and small" to kneel as one before Your throne to say, "God in heaven, forgive us." Make us a great nation, Lord — great only in our desire to know Your truth and walk in Your ways, through Jesus Christ, our Lord. Amen.

Admit It When You're Wrong
Text: 2 Chronicles 34:29-33

And the king stood in his place and made a covenant . . . to walk after the Lord and to keep His commandments. (2 Chronicles 34:31)

I'm going to tell you a true story today, which involves me and a friend of mine named _____.

It happened that one day, I needed a favor from a friend, so I called him up. "Say," I said, "will you pick me up after work tomorrow? I've got to leave my car in the repair shop, and I won't have a way to get home." My friend said, "Sure, no problem. Don't worry about it, and I'll see you tomorrow."

Well, the next day came, and it was raining hard. When work was over, I waited for my friend where I was supposed to meet him, but he never came! Finally, I began walking, and when I got home, I was soaking wet and boiling mad.

I called him up and asked, "Where were you?" Do you know what his answer was? He said, "Hey, it's not my fault; I didn't think of it!" In other words, he had made a promise to me, and he broke it, but it wasn't his fault because he forgot about it!

Now I had two reasons to be mad at him. First, he made me walk home in the rain, and second, he didn't say he was sorry or admit he was wrong. Our friendship suffered because of that, too. Now I knew him as untrustworthy, and I decided I could never ask him for another favor again.

Of course, parents feel just this same way toward their kids. If you do something bad (which I know you hardly ever do!), we parents feel much better about it when you come and tell us what you've done. And from your point of view, if you do something wrong, you would be smart to try and minimize the damage, to make it easier on yourself by admitting it. Remember that "I'm sorry" always sounds much better than "It wasn't my fault!" Don't try to lie about it, cover it up, blame it on someone else or talk your way out of it.

There was a king in Israel named Josiah, and one day he found out he had been doing wrong things in the sight of God. So, he gathered all the people together and admitted what he had done. He promised to change his ways and obey God's law in the future.

This made it easier for God to forgive the king. In fact, the Bible says that God went on to make him a great king. Try to be big enough and brave enough to admit it when you are wrong. It helped King Josiah, and it will help you, too. Amen.

fifth sunday in lent
God Forsaken
Text: Mark 15:22-34

---

*And at the ninth hour, Jesus cried out with a loud voice,
"Eloi, Eloi, la'ma sabach-tha'ni?" which means, "My
God, My God, why hast Thou forsaken Me?"*
(Mark 15:34)

Many churches today read from the Revised Standard Version or the New Revised Standard Version of the Bible, but it wasn't always that way. In fact, the first RSV translation was printed in 1952. There were great arguments within many congregations between those who wanted to accept the new Bible and those who wanted to keep the old King James Bible.

At the height of this controversy, one passionate church member stood up and said, "Keep the old Bible. If the King James English was good enough for Jesus, it's good enough for me!"

You wonder how such a person could have overlooked the verse we find in our text, because here we have Jesus speaking to us in His own tongue. This is one of the few things Jesus said which comes to us undiluted and undefiled by centuries of translation: "Eloi, Eloi, la'ma sabach-tha'ni?"

These words have always had a powerful hold on the imagination of the faithful, because this is just what the witnesses heard at Calvary. In these words, you can hear the Master's voice, you can feel like you were there when they crucified our Lord. "Eloi Eloi, la'ma sabach-tha'ni?"

But more than the authenticity of this verse, there is also the meaning of what Jesus said: "My God, My God, why hast Thou forsaken Me?" He didn't whisper it; He said it in a loud cry. He shouted it out, and He didn't care who heard Him in His moment of pain and doubt.

He said, in effect, "My God, My God, I am so alone. The crowds which once sang My praises and followed My every step have deserted Me. My friends have fled. The soldiers sit here and gamble for the only possessions I own in this world."

"Lord, see how My enemies have come to watch Me die. And see how they are not content to let Me die in peace! They must mock Me, cheer My pain and spit their venomous hatred upon Me. And even You, My heavenly Father, where are You? My God, My God, why hast Thou forsaken Me?"

"Eloi, Eloi, where are You, God?" Most of us suffer at least one moment in life where we want to ask that question ourselves. It comes in the darkest night of the soul, and if you've ever been there, you know exactly what I mean. All seems lost. You feel utterly alone. There seems no reason to go on.

A feeling of helplessness floods the senses, and you are too weak even to stand. You lie there paralyzed and overwhelmed; you hear the voice ringing in your head: "Where are You, God? Why have You forsaken me?"

The truth is that even for Christian believers, life is not always a "Be Happy Attitude." There are times when we feel defeated and forsaken. There are even times when we can want to die, if we tell the truth about it! There are times when we can feel like Jesus; "My God, My God, why hast Thou forsaken Me?"

What does religion say to these tortured people? Do we stand mute in the face of their pain? Do we tell them they are wrong to feel forsaken? Are we supposed to stick a "Smile, God loves you" button on their lapel and let it go at that?

What do you do when you reach the valleys of life, and how do you survive the darkest nights of the soul? How do you go on when all you want to do is lie down and quit?

Some people find strength in stubbornness. They are simply too stubborn to quit. They grit their teeth and say, "I must hold on" — and that's all they know how to do.

Some people are driven by a fear of failure. They don't want to be the kind of person who gives up. Faced with the prospect of crossing the line into permanent defeat, they turn back because they can't bear the thought of being a failure in life.

Some people drive themselves forward by challenging themselves. President John Kennedy talked about this when he first launched our nation's space program, and in light of all that has happened since that time, it is a story worth remembering.

He quoted from a book by Frank O'Conner, an Irish writer. It seems that when O'Connor was a boy, he would take walks through the orchard fields, and sometimes he would come to a wall which looked too high to climb over. But instead of giving up his journey, he would throw his hat over the wall. Then he had no choice but to keep going. President Kennedy used to say that this is what we have done with the space program. We have thrown our hat into space, and now we have no choice but to go after it.

Isn't this precisely how some people overcome the barriers and burdens they meet in life? They propel themselves forward by putting themselves in a position where they have to meet the challenge.

Now, all of this is fine, as far as it goes. But still, we are talking only about our own inner resources. What happens when we lose the strength that stubbornness brings? What happens when the fear of failure has lost its sting, or when we are so beaten down that we can no longer rise to the challenge?

What happens when we feel utterly abandoned and forsaken, even by God? Think of Jesus on the cross. We can endure the pain, the hatred and the mockery. We can even endure being forsaken by our friends. But to feel like you are forsaken by God! Then there is nothing left! Then you feel radically alone! Then there is no point in throwing your hat over the wall because you'll still feel alone when you get to the other side.

For Jesus, this feeling — however brief it was — was surely the "crucifixion within the crucifixion" and "sorrow's crown of sorrow." This surely hurt more than the nails in His hands and feet, or the spear in His side. And for us, there is no darker night, no deeper despair, than to feel God forsaken.

Some of you who are older may remember a schoolbook called the *McGuffey Reader*. (If you don't want to admit that you remember this book, perhaps you will confess you heard your parents speak about it.) But there is a story in that book about a preacher who compared the deaths of Socrates and Jesus. The heart of his sermon was a point he drove home over and over again: "Socrates died like a philosopher; Jesus died like a God."

Well, the preacher was wrong. Jesus didn't die like a God. He died like a man. He was moved to say what we might say: *"Eloi, Eloi, la'ma sabach-tha'ni?"* And therein lies our hope and our strength. By Jesus' cry of forsaken despair, we know that He is with us. We know His light can shine into the darkest corners of the darkest night, to lead us back home again.

When people are filled with dejection,they are often told to put themselves in someone else's shoes, and then they might feel better. But we don't have to do that now, because Christ has already put Himself in our shoes.

He's been where we are; in fact, He's known more of the night than we could ever know. We can never truly say, "I am alone." We can never truly say, "No one understands." "What a Friend we have in Jesus, all our sins and griefs to bear."

It is the distinctive genius of Christianity that we have a God who was also a man. He is not remote and removed from our sufferings. No other religion can say of its God: "Surely He has borne our griefs" (Isaiah 53:4). Surely in our own grief, we are able to ask, and answer the question even as we ask it:

> *Was it for crimes that I had done?*
> *He groaned upon the tree?*
> *Amazing pity! Grace unknown!*
> *And love beyond degree.*

So it is with every trial we may face. No valley is too deep, and no night is too dark because we have a Savior who has already walked that path before us. He is able to be wherever we must be, to give us His "love beyond degree."

By His cry of despair from the cross, Jesus gives us permission to feel our own despair. He tells us not to be ashamed when we feel forsaken, for how can we be ashamed to feel what Jesus felt Himself?

Instead, we are meant to know that out of our defeat comes the victory. Out of our darkness comes the light. Paul says, "I boast of my weakness" (2 Corinthians 12:9). It is in our weakness that Christ gives us the strength to carry on. This is the abiding power of the Christian faith, the enduring message of a God who hung on a cross to die.

Jesus speaks to us today in His own language, but they are words everyone can understand: *"Eloi, Eloi, la'ma sabachtha'ni?"* He knows what it means to feel God forsaken.

But He is the One who says to us, "Fear not." He is the One who says, "Lo, I am with you always, even to the end of the age" (Matthew 28:20). In faith we should know that even from the depths, even when we feel abandoned and helpless, He is already there. He is always there — to let us know we are not alone, and to help us rise again. Amen.

Pastoral Prayer

Most Holy and Gracious God, who is always ready to hear our prayers, even when we are loathe to say them, we pray for those who are walking through the deserts of doubt and despair today:

We pray for those who seek the oasis of new life, and who thirst for the living waters of faith. They know where they have been but don't know where to go. The day is a torment to them and the night is no comfort. Hear our prayers for people in despair.

We pray for those who live in misery at the hands of others . . . for those who suffer injustice, oppression and hunger . . . those who are persecuted and tortured . . . those who are ruthlessly repressed when they take a stand for justice and peace. They wonder when the power of love shall prevail over loveless power, and when righteousness shall rule. Hear our prayers for people who hope against hope that a better world is coming.

We pray for those who seek the oasis of new life, and who thirst for the living waters of faith. They know where they have been but don't know where to go. The day is a torment to them and the night is no comfort. Hear our prayers for people in despair.

We pray for those who live in misery at the hands of others . . . for those who suffer injustice, oppression and hunger . . . those who are persecuted and tortured . . . those who are ruthlessly repressed when they take a stand for justice and peace. They wonder when the power of love shall prevail over loveless power, and when righteousness shall rule. Hear our prayers for people who hope against hope that a better world is coming.

We thank You, dear God, that You have sent Your son, Jesus Christ, to bear our griefs and carry our burdens. Leave us grateful for our crosses in life, grateful that we are walking in the Way of our Savior. Teach us to see His light in even the darkest night, that our perfect faith may drive out all fear. Help us to see Him standing beside us all our days that we may never feel God forsaken. Make us always able to lean on the everlasting arms of Him who is our rest and our hope, through this life and into all eternity. In Jesus' name we pray. Amen.

children's lesson
Telling Jesus What To Do
Text: Mark 15:22-34

So also the chief priests mocked Him . . . saying, "Let the Christ, the King of Israel, come down now from the cross, that we may see and believe." (Mark 15:31-32)

When they crucified Jesus, and as Jesus hung there dying on the cross, some people stood nearby to tease Him: "If you really are the Son of God," they said, "why don't You prove it? Why don't You save Yourself and come down from the cross, so that we may see and believe in You?"

Have you ever said something like that to Jesus? I know I have! When I was about your age, I used to buy baseball cards at the corner drug store, and one day, I was lucky enough to get a very valuable card . . . the card of my number one favorite ballplayer. His card was quite rare, so I was really excited to have it.

I put it very carefully in the back pocket of my blue jeans and walked home, but when I got home, it was gone! I was crushed! I was broken-hearted! I went back looking for it until it was too dark to see, and all the time I said, "Jesus, if you really are God and if You really do love me, You'll help me find this baseball card." I never found it.

Have you ever spoken to Jesus like I did? "Jesus, show me some miracle, show me some sign, so I can believe in you?" Have you ever said, "Jesus, if you really care about me, help me pass this test that I didn't study for." Or, "Jesus, make so-and-so invite me to the dance." "Jesus, if you really love me, tell my parents to let me go to my friend's house tonight." Have you ever put Jesus to the test like this?

We have to be careful when we try to tell Jesus what to do. Yes, it's true that Jesus cares about us and wants to help

59

us every day of our lives, but He may not always give us what we ask for. He may decide that what we are asking for is selfish and silly. He may decide that what we want isn't what we need.

A lot of people try to use Jesus like this. They don't think about what they can do for Jesus; they only think about what Jesus can do for them. Remember that you can't treat Jesus like a little brother or sister . . . like someone you can tell to jump up and take care of something for you. You don't want to come to Jesus saying, "Jesus, let me tell You what I want You to do." Instead, you want to come to Jesus saying, "Lord, You tell me what You want me to do, and I'll try my best to do it." Amen.

palm sunday
Palms By Day And Plots By Night
Old Testament Text: Isaiah 50:4-9a
New Testament Text: John 12:9-19

Who will contend with me? Let us stand up together.
Who is my adversary? Let him come near to me."

(Isaiah 50:8)

I am so glad Jesus lived long enough in the flesh to see
Palm Sunday. He deserved it; you might even say He needed
it. Everyone needs a day like the day Jesus had in Jerusalem.

After spending our lives in thankless toil and turmoil, we
all need at least one day of recognition and praise.

It might come to you as a mother or father on your birth-
day, when the family that always seems to take you for granted
gathers to give you a special gift and a round of applause —
a moment of recognition for all the work you've given them
during the year.

It might come from your place of work, your church, or
some other volunteer organization. After years of commitment
and loyal service, you are rewarded with at least a little bit
of public acclaim. It's nice to be thanked for all your time and
effort.

Brief as it was, Palm Sunday might have felt like that kind
of day to Jesus — He who had known such conflict and controversy all His life. From the day of His infancy when King
Herod tried to butcher Him, to His final agony on Calvary,
Jesus faced more than His share of critics and enemies. His
was a life-long contest with a world which resents goodness
and despises God's Word.

Yes, I imagine Jesus felt some satisfaction as He entered
Jerusalem. Coming down the Mount of Olives, He could see
people lining the narrow, winding road into the valley. Looking

61

up ahead, He could see them cheering by the city gate — the very place where Israel expected the Messiah to come (cf. Joel 3:1-12). I imagine Jesus took this moment of triumph and drank it in: "Hosanna! Hosanna! Blessed is He who comes in the name of the Lord!"

Jesus looked into the faces of the people who pressed around Him. They were smiling; it was a warm, friendly crowd. Joyful hands reached up to touch Him as He rode His donkey. And Jesus saw the children. Children love a parade, and our Lord watched as they ran alongside, laughing and shouting — filled with the boundless energy and excitement that only children have. The crowd was there to celebrate! I'm so glad Jesus lived long enough among us to have a day like this!

Of course, our Lord knew exactly what the people were thinking about as they watched Him enter the city. Many of them were remembering the prophet Zechariah's words:

> *Here comes your King,*
> *Triumphant and victorious,*
> *Humbly riding . . . on the foal of an ass!*
> *He banishes all . . . war-horses from Jerusalem,*
> *His words make peace for the nations,*
> *His sway extends from sea to sea,*
> *From the Euphrates to the ends of the earth.*
>   (Zechariah 9:9-10, Moffatt translation)

"Here is the Messiah who was promised of old," they were thinking. "Here is the One whom God has sent to liberate us and bring us peace! Blessed is He who comes in the name of the Lord!"

The crowd was thinking of Zechariah, but Jesus may have remembered another prophet, Isaiah. Knowing scripture as well as He did, Jesus may well have recalled the very words in our text:

> *The Lord God has opened my ear,*
> *and I was not rebellious . . .*
> *I gave my back to the smiters . . .*
> *I hid not my face from shame and spitting . . .*
> *Who will contend with me? Let us stand up together.*
> *Who are my adversaries? Let them confront me.*

Now, why might Jesus think of Isaiah on this, the day of His biggest triumph? When He is basking in more public acclaim than He's ever known before, why might He think of "adversaries" and "smiters" who wait to stab Him in the back?

Because Jesus knows what is coming. He knows that there are plots being laid against Him in the midst of the palms. He is aware that people are working against Him in secret: "Who will contend with me? Let us stand up together. Who are my adversaries? Let them confront me."

And so it is that somewhere in the crowd, a few guerrilla fighters — revolutionary Zealots — are probably whispering to one another: "See how this Nazarene has the people so excited. He may be just the One we need to lead our fight against Rome. Let us see if we can use Jesus to help our nation's cause."

Roman soldiers and government spies are undoubtedly watching Jesus, and saying to themselves: "They call this Jesus a king! This is dangerous treason; there can be no king but Caesar! (cf. John 19:15). We'd better have someone keep an eye on this Man."

Somewhere in the crowd, Judas is deciding what he will do. He won't go to Jesus directly with his dissatisfactions. He won't even go to the other disciples. Instead, he will sneak off and meet with the authorities in secret. One of Jesus' own leaders! Somewhere in the crowd, Judas is deciding to become a Judas.

Finally, as our text in John's gospel tells us, the Pharisees are looking on and muttering to one another: "You see that [we] can do nothing; look, the whole world has gone after him."

These establishment leaders know that they cannot contend with Jesus face to face. They will have to speak against Him behind His back. They will have to arrest Him after dark, away from the city, and try Him illegally. They'll need false witnesses to testify against Him. Palms by day and plots by night.

Jesus doesn't let the cowardice and secrecy of His enemies go unanswered. When they finally step forward to arrest Him in Gethsemane, He rebukes them: "Have you come out as against a robber, with swords and clubs? When I was with you day after day in the temple, you did not lay your hands on Me. But this is your hour, and the power of darkness" (Luke 22:52-53).

As we see Jesus riding into Jerusalem today, and as we think about all that is to come in the days ahead, it might well seem that Isaiah's words were written just for Him. In effect: "Who will contend with Me? Who will declare Me guilty?" Let them step forward and show themselves! Let them forsake the safety of the shadows for the bright light of day, and be brave enough to do in public what they are so willing to do in private."

Who will contend with you? Who are your adversaries? Isn't there something in the Palm Sunday story that we all experience in our own lives, each in our own way?

The fact is our own adversities in life often plot against us in secret, hidden by shadows. That's the trouble with trouble: it usually doesn't advertise itself. It doesn't come sauntering down the street, look you in the eye and say, "Hello, I'm Trouble, so get ready — I'll be visiting you in a few days."

Instead, life's misfortunes leap out at us from the side of the road. Life's slings and arrows rain down upon us from behind the bushes: "Who are my adversaries? Who is doing this to me? Let them show themselves and come near to me."

When your food stamps are cut, or the plant is shut down, how often do you see the person who made that decision in some far away government office or corporate board room? You want to cry out, "Who did this, and turned my life upside down? What is his name? Where does she live? Let that person come near to me."

When you are victimized by the gossip and false witness of others, you want to know who is saying these terrible things about you, and why they won't come forward and say them to your face. It's maddening, because you can't fight the shadows! "Who will contend with me? Let us stand up together."

But it's not just other people striking at us from behind closed doors; our adversaries can simply be the circumstances of life. I mean: who knows what tomorrow will bring? Who wakes up in the morning knowing that the phone will ring that day: "I'm sorry, Mr. So-and-so; there's been a terrible accident . . ." I know, because I've gotten that phone call. It hits you like a punch in the gut, and you never see it coming.

What about the demons so many of us carry inside? What about the regrets we have — of the things we wish we had done, or the things we wish we hadn't done? They're invisible! They live in the shadows and strike at our weakest point! The preacher can speak a thousand times about God's grace and forgiveness, but still the demons live. "Who are my adversaries? Let them come near to me. Let me see them face to face, that I may finally be free of their torment."

And so it is with what probably matters the most to us: our health. When we fall and break our arm, we can see the cast we wear, and we know it is coming off in a matter of weeks. It's the problems we can't see that terrify us — the cancers, the viruses, the mysterious diseases. "Who will contend with me? Let me see you, that I may know what you are."

Palms by day and plots by night. That's just how it is in life. It's frustrating when you have to contend with shadows. It's frustrating when your adversaries won't stand up with you, and come near to show you who they are. It hurts when life's troubles trip us from behind and send us sprawling.

So it was with Jesus on that Palm Sunday road. In the midst of the palms and the cheering crowds, our Lord might well have heard Isaiah's words in His heart. But if Jesus heard Isaiah speak of "smiters" and "adversaries," He also heard the rest of what the prophet said:

For the Lord helps me;
therefore, I have not been confounded . . .
that I know I shall not be put to shame;
[for] He who vindicates me is near.

We ought to remember this as we make our way on the highways and byways of life. Jesus' experience of Palm Sunday suggests that life rarely gives pure, unblemished triumphs. Achievement and adversity often come hand in hand. If there are palms by day, there are also plots by night.

But even when trouble leaps out of nowhere to stab us in the back, we do best by keeping our face set forward — looking toward God. It doesn't matter whether it's other people or just the circumstances of life: adversaries win the battle, but God wins the war. Adversaries surprise, but God sustains. Life is not always fair, but our fairest Lord Jesus is always there to be our strength and our salvation.

There are times in life when we might feel like crying out, "Who will contend with me? Let us stand up together. Who are my adversaries? Let them come near to me." But then we must also be able to say: "[Behold], the Lord God helps me and I know I shall not be put to shame, [for] He who vindicates me is near."

Jesus has taken that path before us, and He invites us now to follow behind. Do it as He did it so long ago, on that bright, sunny day in Jerusalem. He went forward resolutely, fully aware of the trouble He faced, but His eyes were set firmly on the greater glory yet to come. Amen.

Pastoral Prayer

Gracious and Ever-Merciful God, who has come to us in the flesh, in the Person of Jesus Christ, that You might share our burdens and lighten the yokes we must carry in this world, we pray for all who are anxious about their lives. We pray for those who wonder what they shall eat, or where they shall find clothes to wear, or how they shall care for their families. We pray for those who are ill of body or spirit, those who are troubled of conscience, and those who hunger and thirst for something to believe in. Be with all the people in our prayers, O Lord, that every heart may know Your grace and every lip may praise Your name, and all Your people may live in the fullness and goodness of life.

Everlasting God, who comes into our hearts today riding on a humble donkey, but who lives and reigns forever as King of kings and Lord of lords, keep us strong when life is unfair. Give us courage to turn our backs to the smiters, and even when they contend with us from the shadows, let us look to You always as our Light along the way. When we are made fearful by the twists and turns and unpleasant surprises of life, comfort our troubled hearts and quicken our weary spirits, that we may walk firmly and righteously all the days of our lives, and even to eternal life. Through Jesus Christ our Lord. Amen.

children's lesson
Will You Try Another Way?
Text: Isaiah 50:4-9

I gave my back to the smiters . . .

(Isaiah 50:6a)

Does anyone know what a "smiter" is? *(Let them answer.)* What would you do if you met a smiter? *(Let them answer again.)*

A smiter is someone who hits you — hard. So you see, what I'm asking is: what would you do if someone came up and hit you as hard as they could? You would have some choices, wouldn't you.

First, if someone hit you, you could take our your "secret invisible megatransformulator ray gun" and zap the person away. Well, you can't really do that, of course — life isn't like a cartoon, so we'll need to find some other response.

Second, if someone hit you, you could go get someone else who is bigger and stronger, to come and beat up the person who hit you. Or third, you could decide to beat up the person yourself; if someone hit you, you could hit back and get into a fight.

The Bible teaches another way. In the Old Testament, a man named Isaiah said, "I gave my back to the smiters . . ." Then Jesus said, "Turn the other cheek" (Matthew 5:39). In other words, if someone hits you, turn your back to them! Turn the other cheek and let him hit you again! That's what the Bible teaches, and what Jesus wants us to do.

Of course, most people don't think Jesus' way can really work. Most adults don't believe it — even most Christian adults don't believe it — that's why we have so many wars in this world. And most kids don't believe in Jesus' way either. Most people think that if someone hits you, you have to hit back

— answer force with force — take an eye for an eye and a tooth for a tooth.

But try to think about this today. Suppose you hit me, right here in the face. Then suppose I turned the other cheek to let you hit me again. Would you be able to do it? Would you be able to hit me again when I wasn't even trying to defend myself?

Some people could, I suppose; but many people could not keep hitting me. If I turn the other cheek to you and you back down, then I have used my power to make you stop, and I have won the victory. I have defeated you without anger or violence. That is the power, the courage and the strength Jesus told us about, the power of nonviolence, the power of love over hate.

It goes against everything we are taught in this world, from cartoons for kids to war games for grown-ups. But we've already seen what happens with the other way, the way of violence. We've seen the gangs on the streets, the fights in school and wars all over the world. The way of violence doesn't work! All it does is breed more violence, and more fear of violence.

There is another way — the Bible's way — Jesus' way. It is the way of peace, the way of love, the only way to turn your enemies into friends. What about you? You've seen what happens when people hate and hurt and argue and fight with one another. Will you be faithful to Jesus? Will you try another way? Amen.

maundy thursday (communion)
On The Night He Was Betrayed
Text: Mark 14:17

And when it was evening, He came with the twelve.
(Mark 14:12-16)

We are gathered here in the evening, after the sun is down, so perhaps we can use the darkness around us to better imagine the events which took place on this sacred night so long ago.

The story actually begins earlier in the day, when Jesus sends two disciples into Jerusalem to make preparations for the Passover meal. You may remember a sermon from a few weeks ago ("The Boy Who Ran Away") in which I mentioned that Jesus has to use an "underground" organization and secret signals to get safely around Jerusalem in these last days. In this case, the signal is a man carrying a jug of water — he is a secret sympathizer who will lead the disciples to the Upper Room. With spies and informers around every corner, Jesus and His friends can't be too careful as they prepare to enter Jerusalem on Maundy Thursday night.

Once the two disciples find this man and follow him to the Upper Room, it remains for Jesus and the twelve to come into the city. They wait until it is dark, and then they begin the twenty-minute walk down the Mount of Olives. They follow the winding road into the shadows of the Kidron valley and up the hill to Jerusalem, until they pass through the gate and enter the city.

The Mount of Olives and the Garden of Gethsemane lie to the east of the city, while the house which contained the Upper Room is on the southwestern side. This means that Jesus and His disciples had to walk all the way through the city along its twisting, narrow streets. He probably took a longer route than necessary in order to avoid passing near Pilate's temple guards.

If you've ever walked those streets in the old city of Jerusalem (particularly on a dark night), you know that they are a labyrinth, a complete mystery to all but the native born. It takes just a few minutes to get hopelessly lost in their maze. I'm sure, however, that Jesus walked briskly and knew exactly where He was going on that final, fateful night.

The city streets are no more than ten feet wide, bounded to the left and right by the walls of the houses, which border right on the edge of the street. As you come near the location of the Upper Room, you climb a number of steps which are built into the street. Jesus and the twelve kept walking up these steps until they reached the particular house which held the Upper Room.

They did not eat the Last Supper sitting at a table, as Leonardo da Vinci has painted it — that was a European custom. Instead, they followed Middle Eastern practice and lay on the floor before a three-sided table which sat low to the ground.

At some point during the meal, Jesus said that one of His disciples would betray Him. You can imagine the uproar and confusion which ensued, as the disciples all clamored to find out who it was: "Is it I, Lord?" They heard His chilling words: "[Concerning the one who is to betray Me], It would have been better for that man if he had not been born."

It might be useful on some other occasion to speculate on why Judas did it. For now, let me just say that Christ is most often betrayed not by outsiders who are enemies of the faith, but by Christians themselves. More harm is done to the cause of Christ by Christians who don't practice their faith or are tragically confused about its content, than is ever done by non-Christians bent on destroying the church from the outside. This pattern of "insider" betrayal began with Judas and continues to this day. That is why all of us must ask the question tonight: "Is it I, Lord; is it I?"

Jesus also took time on this Maundy Thursday night to wash His disciples' feet — a ritual which many churches are also performing tonight. Jesus gave His disciples a vivid reminder, a living parable for the servant life He was calling them to. Maundy Thursday is a good time to remember that we get it all wrong if we come to faith or come to the church asking what we can get out of it. The better question is: what can we give? By washing His disciples' feet, Jesus is telling us that to be His disciple, we should worry more about serving than being served.

Then Jesus came to that part of the meal which has become our sacrament, the sacrament of the Lord's Supper. In taking the Passover bread as He did, He hearkened back to the early days of Israel — back to the ancient law as given in Deuteronomy, where the unleavened bread is called the "bread of affliction" (16:3). Surely this was in Jesus' mind as He said the words which have become so familiar to us today: "Take this bread and eat, for this is My body which is broken for you . . ."

Pay attention to those words when you hear them said tonight, because they contain an important lesson for faith. Tonight, Jesus is telling us to "take" what He is giving us. On other occasions and elsewhere in the gospels, He has told us to "follow" Him, and surely the Christian life involves our effort to imitate Him and follow in His ways as best we can.

But before we can do that, we first have to receive. We have to receive His love and His mercy as a gift — not as something we earn. The message is there in our communion words: "Take this bread and eat . . . Take this cup and drink . . ." Take this faith which Jesus Christ is freely giving you tonight.

One more aspect of this Maundy Thursday night stands out, as Mark's gospel has presented it in our text this evening. It is that Jesus gave thanks — twice — and that He sang a hymn with the disciples before they left for the Mount of Olives.

Think about that for a moment. On the night He was betrayed, Jesus gave thanks. He sang a hymn. It shows that the faithful heart is never defeated. It shows that the world can take your body, your money, your health and whatever else; but only you can give it your spirit. Jesus kept His spirit until the end.

Someone has said that death was waiting outside the door as Jesus broke bread and shared the cup, but God was inside the door. Jesus knew that He could rely on God completely, not just to get Him through the ease of the day, but also through the terrors of the night. Trust in God for everything, and you will always have reason to be thankful. You will always have reason to rejoice, just as Jesus did on the night He was betrayed. Amen.

good friday
The Victory Of The Cross
Old Testament Text: Psalm 139:7-12
New Testament Text: Luke 23:44-49

*. . . and there was darkness over the whole land until the
ninth hour.* (Luke 23:44b)

In the rolling hills of northern New Jersey stands a small
church with a large, stone cross cut into an inside wall. Now,
it happened that one of the church's wealthier members didn't
like the cross there and said it was an eyesore. He offered to
give a huge donation to the church in order to take the cross
out of the wall and replace it with a stained glass window.

But when he presented his idea to the church's leaders, they
said to him, "We cannot do what you ask. The architect
designed the church to have this cross; it gives strength to the
wall. If you take away the cross, you will destroy the church."

In the church I attended as a boy, they brought a big, plain
wooden cross into the sanctuary one year during Lent, and
for five Sundays, they drove nails into it to symbolize the sins
that killed Jesus. I can still hear the sound of those nails being pounded into the wood. And I remember overhearing one
woman complain about it: "That cross is so barren and bare;
it upsets the beauty of the church. I wish they would take it
away."

But the cross stayed in my boyhood church, just as it stayed
in the wall of that church in New Jersey. When you take away
the cross, you destroy the Christian church.

Other religions have symbols which suggest beauty and
light: the six-pointed star of Judaism, the crescent moon of
Islam, the lotus symbol of Buddhism. But the Christian symbol is a cross — a sign of savage brutality, an instrument of
capital punishment. Alone among the world's religions, the

the symbol of Christianity is:

> *an old rugged cross,*
> *the emblem of suffering and shame.*

And there is something about this symbol which has always been difficult and upsetting to many people. We would rather look into the light of a stained glass window than stare into the dark agony and sacrifice of Calvary. We would rather keep our churches pure and clean than be reminded of the human cruelty and messy ugliness which are represented in the cross. We'd rather practice a pseudo-Easter religion than deal with Good Friday lives in a Good Friday world.

Paul called the cross a "stumbling block" and a "folly" (1 Corinthians 1:23), and so it has always been. It is hard to comprehend that God Himself would come to our world and be put to death in such a way. We shrink back from the thought, but the essential truth remains: take away that blood-soaked cross of suffering and shame, and all our faith is in vain.

Jesus was often asked, "What must I do to gain eternal life?" "O Master, when you ascend to Your Father in heaven, may I sit at Your right hand in glory?" And Jesus always had a similar answer: "Are you ready to deny yourself and pick up your cross and follow Me?" "Are you willing to drink the cup of betrayal down to the last bitter dregs for My sake?"

These questions from Jesus are best answered in the abstract, because when we think of how He was actually crucified, the cost of discipleship becomes too much to bear. O precious Jesus, sinless Jesus — how bitter was the cup You drank on our behalf? How much of the world's cruelty and sadistic fury did You endure for us? How deep was Your sorrow,

> *O Sacred Head, now wounded*
> *With grief and shame weighed down,*
> *Now scornfully surrounded*
> *With thorns Thine only crown . . .*

76

The cup Jesus drank was as bitter as worldly power could devise. After all, a Roman crucifixion was more than a mere execution. It was an elaborate ritual meant to defeat the mind and shatter the spirit even as it destroyed the body.

First, there was the scourging. Jesus was stripped naked and tied to a post. The whip they used on Him was made of leather and for extra pain, small nails were embedded into the tips of the thongs. They whipped Him nearly to death, and His blood was flowing like rivulets from His wounds.

Then came the mockery, the "sore abuse and scorn." This was especially gratifying to the soldiers, who didn't like being assigned duty in the hot, unfriendly climate of Israel. The chance to mock a prisoner, to humiliate him and play with his mind before killing him, this was good for the soldiers' morale.

It began with something called the "King's Game" — a sort of "board game" carved into the pavement (John 19:13) of the Judgment Hall. You can still see that hall in Jerusalem, and the exact spot on the pavement where soldiers played this game to mock their prisoner, as our Lord stood by in suffering silence.

Next, because Jesus was charged with being a king, they put a robe on Him and drove a crown of thorns into His scalp. Then they spit on Him and poured out their scorn: "Hail, O mighty Jesus! Caesar shakes in his boots over You! Watch as we kneel before You, You pitiful, laughable King! Tell us: where are your subjects now? Who will save You now from the power of Rome?"

When the mockery was done, they dragged Jesus out to the city street and tied the short beam of the cross to His back. The long beam was waiting for Him at Calvary. So bitter was to be His defeat that He would carry His own instrument of death to the place of His execution.

There was a crowd following Jesus, and more people waiting outside the city walls, on Calvary. Most were there for the spectacle. As in our own day, when there is an execution in one of our prisons, a crowd often gathers outside the prison wall to cheer when the deed is done. Well, that same kind of crowd came to watch Jesus die, and they cheered when He appeared at the city gate, staggering up the hill to the "place of the skull."

When Jesus got to Calvary, they took His robe off once again. As artists have painted the scene, Jesus has a piece of linen around His waist but in actual fact, the victim was made to die completely naked in front of all the people. Also, the law required that crucifixions be done next to a busy highway. This was done to humiliate the prisoner even further, and to serve as a public warning to others against violating Roman law and order.

Next, they put the cross together and made Him lie down upon it. A cheer rose up from the crowd as they drove the nails into His wrists. Again, most of the pictures you see show the nails piercing His hands, but crucifixions weren't done like that. The nails would have ripped right through the fleshy part of the hand once He was put upright, so they fastened Jesus more securely by driving the nails between the bones in the wrist.

The crowd cheered again as they drove the nail into His feet. "Crucify Him!" To make sure He wouldn't fall off the cross, the soldiers placed a small platform beneath Him. Now He could hang there indefinitely, to die as slowly as He could.

A hush came over the crowd as the cross was pulled upright and dropped into the hole in the ground. This is what they had come to see! As the cross dropped into the ground, a searing, excruciating pain ran through Jesus' body. And as a final mockery — a final indignity — the charge against Him was inscribed on a sign and placed over His head: "This is the King of the Jews."

Now, began the slow ordeal of helpless, agonizing death. Passers-by along the highway stopped to stare before moving on. Some jeered at Him, telling Him to come down off the cross and save Himself, if He really was the Christ (Matthew 27:39f).

Jesus' mother and the other women stood to the side, overcome by grief. And as for the soldiers, they sat on the ground near the cross to gamble and while the hours away. They joked about how well this prisoner was withstanding the punishment and compared Him to other prisoners they had killed in this manner.

But this was no ordinary execution. This was a divine drama, a moment of eternity come to earth. The sky began to darken. The birds of the air stopped singing; the flowers began to fold back into their buds. The people looked up in confusion and fear. Something was wrong! All of nature was upset! All of nature was involved in the event at Calvary.

What manner of darkness was this? It was deeper than the darkness which terrifies a child waking up in the middle of the night. It was deeper than the dark sins which blot your heart and mine, the sins for which Jesus died. It was deeper than the darkness of the crowd's bloodlust — the bloodlust which cried, "Crucify Him!" and which cheered as the soldiers inflicted suffering and shame.

This darkness was even deeper than the darkness of Rome — the darkness of dictators and terrorists, nuclear missiles and corporate sweat shops. This was darker than all the abuses of authority by all the powers and principalities of this world.

This was "darkness upon the face of the deep" (Genesis 1:2), the darkness of all hope leaving the world. The sacred head was wounded; the salvation of the world was dying! "There was darkness over the whole land until the ninth hour." It was an utter darkness — unimaginable, unspeakable darkness.

But then, out of the darkness came a voice — not a soft or timid voice, but a loud cry. Not a sigh of defeat but a shout of victory: "It is finished! [It is completed]! Father, into Thy hands I commit My spirit!"

A cry of victory. The victory of the cross. It is a mystery, a stumbling block, a folly. An emblem of suffering and shame is now a symbol of triumph. An instrument of death becomes the ultimate affirmation of life. Out of "sore abuse and scorn" comes the final, unanswerable proof of the Psalmist's faith:

> *Whither shall I go from Thy Spirit? . . .*
> *Even the darkness is not dark to Thee,*
> *The night is as bright as the day;*
> *for darkness is as light with Thee.*

Think now for a moment about what this victory means, this victory of the cross. Why did Jesus endure all of this, and why did we endure hearing it today?

It is, first of all, a victory over sin.

Without the cross, Christianity would be just a set of demands no one could fulfill, since no one is free from the sin which put Jesus Christ to death. "Love your neighbor as yourself. Seek first the Kingdom of God. Give up all you have and follow Me. Be perfect as your Father in heaven is perfect."

Who among us can do this? These are impossible commandments! But now our sin is no longer a barrier. Now we no longer need rely upon our own devices to bring ourselves to God, since by the grace of the cross, God has brought Himself to us.

Many people do not understand this, and it leaves them in great spiritual sorrow. They are tragically burdened by their sin and sorely afflicted by their suffering.

If only they could accept the gift of victory which Christ won for them on the cross! If only they could turn their sin and sorrow over to Jesus — they would find that His yoke is easy and His burden is light! Let all of us accept this victory today! After everything He has endured for us, nothing about our lives could be too heavy for Him to carry, He who has all our sins and grief to bear.

The victory of the cross is also a victory over the world. The Romans were sure they had defeated Christ as they watched Him die on the cross. They were sure that Rome was the power and the glory forever. They didn't realize that their world was dying even as Jesus died, and a new world was being born — a world in which Rome and all the Romes to come would some day pass away.

The guiding beliefs of the Roman Empire are not unfamiliar to us today — love and justice do not count in the world, only force and power. Might makes right and self-interest is supreme. The strong attack the weak and the rich abuse the poor. So it is in a world racing headlong down the path of destruction.

If only we could see the new world which Christ has begun at Calvary! If only we could see that despite all appearances to the contrary, the future belongs to God! Now we know that when brute force and worldly power have spoken, God's love and justice will have the final Word. This is also the victory of the cross.

The victory of the cross is so complete that it even marks victory over death, that final darkness and common denominator, that one inescapable reality. Here we find our greatest fears, yet even here, God has the final Word! The cross is an instrument of death. It is also the ultimate proof of life.

If we could just grasp this, we could truly live our lives from beginning to end in fullness and grace. We could live with the song on our lips, "O grave, where is thy victory; death, where is thy sting?" O what strength and confidence is ours by Christ's victory over death! This is freedom in its deepest sense — freedom bought and paid for by the victory of the Cross.

• • •

I spent quite some time in this sermon describing the crucifixion in all its gory detail. I wanted us to be spectators, witnesses to that terrible event. I did this for a reason. If we suffer to see His agony, we may also know His victory.

I learned in my boyhood church that the cross must always be the center of our Christian faith. Take it away, and you destroy the church and all it stands for. Take away the cross, and you take away the victory of the cross Christ has given each of us.

This will always be a stumbling block and a folly, even to many Christians. We want stained glass windows in our churches; we want to hear about blessings and promises. But those blessings and those promises came at a price. We celebrate an Easter religion, but we must live in a Good Friday world.

It may be barren and plain, it may be painful and ugly to look at, and it might speak too much truth to bear about ourselves and the world we live in. But never hesitate to "Go to dark Gethsemane." Cling always to that old rugged cross, that emblem of suffering and shame. In Christ, the victory is won. Death becomes life, and a cross is exchanged for a crown. Amen.

Pastoral Prayer

Gracious God, whose Son, Jesus, knows the depths of our sorrows better than we can know them ourselves, we pray for those who are troubled or afflicted of body or spirit today:

. . . for those whose loved ones are far away, and who yearn for the day when no distance shall come between them;

. . . for those who are ill or in pain, and who yearn for the day of healing and release;

. . . for those who need Your company, O God, but cannot find it. Heal their emptiness, and fill them with Your Word, that their cup may runneth over, and they may dwell in the house of the Lord forever.

Heavenly God, who came to our world as a suffering servant, hear our prayers for all who need the victory of the cross today. By that victory, purchased with His pain and blood, give us the confidence to live in Your ways. Give to us the security of knowing that Yours is the final word, over every manner of darkness and even over death. Give to us the joy and freedom of living in a new world, starting today — a world which was begun on that hill so far away. We pray in thankful remembrance today, thankful for the victory which Jesus won at Calvary. Amen.

easter sunday (early service)
The Message Of The Morning Light
Text: 2 Corinthians 5:16-21

*Therefore if anyone is in Christ, there is a new creation;
the old has passed away, behold, the new has come.*
(2 Corinthians 5:17)

Just as a handful of women and disciples came early in the day to the garden tomb, so do Christians come out early on this Easter Sunday to find the empty grave. Let us try to recapture the original wonder, the original excitement they felt on that special day so long ago. Let us imagine that God is speaking directly to us this morning, down through the heavens and deep into our hearts, giving us the message of the morning light.

●　●　●

"You see how the stone has been rolled away," says the Lord our God, "and you wonder what it means. Behold, the old creation which I made for you has passed away, and now the new has come. See how much I loved the world, that I gave my only begotten Son, who now lives and reigns for ever more."

"I have torn down the greatest barrier which stood between you and Me. From now on, you need regard no one from a human point of view. From now on, you may see all things, even death itself, in a brand new way. All of this is the meaning of the empty tomb you see this morning."

"Your time on earth is short and your memories even shorter, but My time and My memory go on forever; so I will tell you how you came to this place this morning. Listen carefully. Be still and hear My words, and know that I am God."

83

"In the beginning, I created the heavens and the earth. I filled the earth with everything you need to survive and prosper, and then I created you. Male and female, I made you in My own image. Do not think you look like Me, for no one has seen the face of God. No, the image you share with Me, which you have seen but through a glass darkly, is seated in your soul."

"I set before you the ways of life and death, and you chose the ways of death. From the very earliest day, as soon as you knew the difference between good and evil, you chose your own way. You wrote your history with the blood spilled by Cain. It was through your own freedom to choose evil that sin and death came into the world. You are Adam, and you are Eve."

"Yet I did not turn My back on you. When I despaired of all your sin and violence and nearly destroyed the world because of you, I let the faithfulness of Noah preserve you. When you cried out as Pharaoh's slaves, I sent fearless leaders to take you to the Promised Land. I showed you many signs and wonders. I gave you My law, that you might know My ways and build a beloved community in My sight, a light to all the nations of the earth."

"But still you pursued your own selfish advantage over one another. Still you divided yourselves and hated each other by race and clan and creed. I told you that by My law there would be no poor among you, and behold: you have filled the land with your poor and oppressed! You have stubbornly sought your own gods, thinking that they will satisfy your longings, instead of receiving life in all its fruitful abundance in obedience to My will."

"Even then, I kept pursuing you, involving Myself in your affairs. I sent prophets to speak in My name, to tell you of the new heart and new spirit I would put within you. And when they spoke harsh words to you, it was for your own good, that you may return to Me and repent of your wickedness and faithlessness."

"Still, you did not listen; you persecuted My prophets instead. When you cast them out of your cities and threw them into pits, you defied Me and defiled My truth, which was spoken to you in love. I have endured much on your account."

"But I am God, and God is love, and My love for you cannot be shaken. Finally, I decided that the hearing of My Word was not enough for you. At last, I decided that I must come and be with you Myself, that you might understand Me better in the human form most familiar to you. I came to shatter the limits of your moral imagination and reveal to you the Way to your salvation."

"Maybe, in your false piety and empty worship, you thought you would honor My arrival with fanfare and trumpets. I came quietly, in a manger. Maybe you expected a king on a throne. I came as a servant. I showed you by My birth and in the whole manner of My living that My ways are not your ways. I walked your streets and visited your homes, teaching and admonishing and healing you in body and spirit, showing you at every moment what I look like in your own flesh and blood."

"I came to you knowing how you would receive Me: knowing you would reject Me and send Me to Calvary. Still I persisted, suffering all on your account, completing My chosen course."

"And now look what I have done! Though you killed Me, yet do I live! Though you crucified your only Hope, yet have I returned to you. Is this not how I said it would be?"

"Today, I have offered you more than you can ever imagine. Give up all you think you need, and receive more than you could ever desire. Be ready to die to all that is in you for the love of the world, and live for evermore in the love of your God."

"When you are burdened with the sorrow and the pity and the anxieties of this life, trust in Me; for I have shown you all along that I am always there. When you feel alone, distant and cut off from Me; know that it is I who came to you in the flesh, to remove all distance and break all barriers between us."

"When you despair of the ways of this world — when you cry out in anguish at the injustice and poverty and bloodshed which never cease — put your faith in Me, for I have overcome the world. I have revealed to you the first fruits of My kingdom. Wait with patient hope for what you cannot see, but see in My Risen Son that the love of injustice and the grinding of the face of the poor and the spilling of blood must someday pass away."

"And when you contemplate the end of your earthly days, let not your hearts be troubled, neither let them be afraid; for the grave no longer has its victory, nor death its sting any more. I have shown you that your earthly life is but a small part of the life I have given you. I have shown you how I take you to My own house with many mansions, which no human hands have built."

"By the empty tomb, do you believe at last in the power of the Lord your God? No longer are you bound by your misuse of My first creation, for I have overcome the wages of your sin. Now you are the new Adam and the new Eve. You are My ambassadors — I who have not counted your trespasses against you. I have reconciled you to Myself, and given to you the ministry of reconciliation."

"Now you must respond. Now it is time to open your hearts to Me, to become My righteousness and live as My people born again."

"Take the love I have shown you and share it with all, offering freely what you have freely received. Take My Risen Spirit within you and give it to a sinking world. Take the light of faith out from under your bushel and put it on a stand — let your light shine, which dark death itself cannot put out. Take to heart the living of My commandments, that by My grace and by your words and deeds, you might now build the new creation which I have begun for you this day."

"So, seek Me no longer among the dead, but among the living. Seek Me no longer in far off places, that you should ask where you must go to find Me, for I am very near to you, even in your hearts and minds. Know that now there is

nothing to separate you from the love of God in Christ Jesus.''
Blessed are you who come today to celebrate the death of death! Blessed are you who hear and see and believe the message of the morning light. Amen.

Is It Hard To Believe?
Texts: Luke 24:1-12; 1 Corinthians 15:12-22

If Christ has not been raised, then our preaching is in vain, and all your faith is in vain.

(1 Corinthians 15:14)

When Jesus was asked to heal a boy who had suffered seizures since his birth, our Lord said to the boy's father, "All things are possible to those who believe." And the boy's father said to Jesus, "I believe; help Thou my unbelief" (Mark 9:23-24).

I wonder how many of us want to say those words as we come to the empty tomb this Easter morning: "Lord, I believe; help Thou my unbelief." Is there anything more difficult for the Christian than believing — really knowing in your heart of hearts — that Jesus Christ rose from the dead?

Do you find it hard to believe this morning? Are you one of those who says today, "Lord, I believe; help Thou my unbelief?"

If you are, don't think you are alone. And don't think you have doubts simply because ours is a modern, technological world. No, we are entirely too impressed with ourselves today. We imagine we are so much more sophisticated and less superstitious than people of ancient times, but the truth is: they found it just as hard to believe in the Resurrection as we find it today.

All you have to do is read the gospels, and see that even the disciples didn't believe the news they heard. Even the disciples doubted the Resurrection! Here in our text from Luke, for example, the disciples called it an "idle tale" (24:11)

When Mary Magdalene came to the empty tomb, her first thought was that someone had stolen the body (John 20:2).

89

When Peter saw the tomb, Scripture says he "wondered" at it; he couldn't figure out what had happened (Luke 24:12). Thomas wouldn't believe until he could touch Jesus' wounds (John 20:25).

And quite obviously, many in the early church thought that the Resurrection stretched the limits of rational understanding, since Paul found it necessary to write in 1 Corinthians: "Now if Christ is preached as raised from the dead, how can some of you say that there is no resurrection of the dead?"

There were other gospels and testimonies being circulated in the early church besides the ones we have in our Bible. There was a Gospel of Mary, a Gospel of Peter, a Gospel of Thomas, and dozens of others. And some of these other gospels tried to "water down" the meaning of the Resurrection, much as we might do today. They said that Jesus didn't actually rise up from the tomb — when Jesus died, he died. What is important, they said, is that the spirit and the teachings of Jesus live on, and that people can experience Him in their own hearts today.

But from its very earliest days, the church insisted on an actual, physical Resurrection. They insisted that Jesus rose *bodily* from the grave. In fact, Paul put the matter as plainly as it can be put: "If Christ has not been raised, then our preaching is in vain, and all your faith is in vain."

Everything depends upon the Resurrection. You might know the Law and recite the Ten Commandments by heart. You might pray to God daily and earnestly strive to love your neighbor as yourself. You might be known far and wide as a living saint, a real credit to the church. But in the end, the whole Christian religion hinges on one question, and one question only: was Jesus Christ actually raised from the dead?

If you find it hard to believe, then I will try to help you with your unbelief today. I will speak to you of faith, where finally, the question ends. But first, let's approach it with some logic. Let us begin by asking ourselves: how can we logically explain what really happened on Easter morning?

If you think about it, there are only four possible explanations. The first is that the enemies of Jesus took His body after it was laid in the tomb.

I can't imagine why the Romans or the high priests would do this, since they held Jesus in such contempt — witness the way they treated Him at His death! But suppose they did take the body, for whatever reason? Then, as the gospel of Jesus Christ began to spread, they only had to produce the body. All they had to do was say, "Look! Here is the body of the Man you say is risen." Their struggle with the Christian church would have been over; the gospel of Jesus Christ would have died then and there.

We know for a fact that the early church was sorely persecuted, first by the Jewish authorities and then by the Romans. Both saw the church as a threat, and the emperor Nero even blamed Christians for the fire which destroyed Rome in 64 A.D. If these enemies of Jesus did have the body, they surely would have produced it and put an end to a church which they considered dangerous and subversive.

The second explanation is that Jesus' friends took His body from the tomb. We know the high priests were worried about this: Matthew's gospel tells us that they went to Pilate and asked that a guard be put on the grave. "Make the grave secure," they said, "lest His followers claim He has risen from the dead, and this last fraud will be worse than the first" (27:64).

But suppose you think Matthew made that up? Then there is still this question: why would the disciples die for a fraud? If they really did steal the body, then they knew they were perpetrating a hoax, and who will willingly die for a hoax?

Again, we know that the early Christians suffered unto death for their faith, and they didn't die easily or painlessly. They were crucified. They were burned. They were ripped apart by lions for the amusement of the Colosseum crowd.

Now, people will die for an idea, like Socrates, who died for the idea of philosophical freedom. People will die for a cause, like Nathan Hale, who said, "I only regret I have but one life to give for my country." But who will die for a hoax? Who will die for someone who is already dead?

The strongest proof of the Resurrection is the witness of the Christian martyrs. They obviously thought they had seen the Risen Christ in the flesh, and not just a ghost or an hallucination. There is no other way to explain their willingness to joyfully suffer and die for what they believed.

A third possibility was discussed in a book some years back, where the author tried to prove that Jesus was still alive when they took Him off the Cross. The book argued that Jesus arranged to take a drug which made Him appear dead, and then He was taken away somewhere to live out His normal life.

But again you have to ask: who would die for a fraud? Do you really think Peter and James and all the others would willingly be martyred for someone who had faked His own execution?

There is another problem with this explanation. We know that the Romans were ruthlessly efficient in crucifixions. They did it often and knew what they were doing. Moreover, Mark's gospel says that Pilate made certain Jesus was dead before he gave the body to Joseph of Arimathea for burial (15:45), which is entirely consistent with what we know about Roman crucifixions. It was customary for the soldiers to periodically check a prisoner on the cross, and if he was taking too long to die, they would break his legs to make him die more quickly.

The Romans couldn't have been fooled. They were simply too experienced, too cruel, and too thorough to believe that they would let Jesus come down from the Cross alive and breathing.

If Jesus was really dead on the Cross, and if neither His enemies nor His friends took the body from the tomb, there is only one other possible explanation — that Jesus rose from the dead just like the gospels say He did.

There are other details given in the gospels which suggest that Easter happened just the way the Bible says it happened.

First, there is the matter of women. Women in that day were not even second-class citizens; they were property. They had little public credibility, yet the first testimony to the Risen Christ was given by a woman. More than that, the woman was Mary Magdalene, a former prostitute! If the gospel writers were concocting a story, and if they wanted to appeal to the strict moral sensibilities of their world, don't you think they would have had a man — and a righteous man at that — as the first witness to the Resurrection?

And what of the disciples, the pillars of the early church? They were too scared to go out to the tomb, and when Mary came back with the news, they clearly did not believe her.

Now, the people who write history have a way of making themselves look good. Read the memoirs of former presidents or famous industrialists and see how they take credit for the good things that happened and blame someone else for the bad. But here in the gospels, the disciples are not at all heroic! We can only conclude that they told the story just as it really happened.

Jesus Christ was raised from the dead. Consider, also, that the cost of *not* believing is enormous. Everything depends upon the Resurrection, and on knowing that it is true.

Paul says that if Christ has not been raised, then he, Paul, is a fraud, a charlatan and a hustler. Every Christian preacher who ever lived — including the one who offers you this sermon now — is a fraud if Christ was not raised from the dead.

If Jesus Christ has not been raised from the tomb, then the enemies of Christ win. Rome wins. There is no hope for the world — we are doomed to wars without ceasing and injustice without end. Only the strong shall survive, and the meek shall never inherit the earth. If Jesus Christ has not been raised from the tomb, there is no morality worth believing in, and history belongs to the forces of darkness.

If Jesus Christ has not been raised from the tomb, says Paul, then all your faith is in vain. Your faith is shallow and empty, for what else can you believe in but Jesus Christ?

Can you believe for one minute that human goodness, or scientific progress, or better education will set this world right? Can you believe in political morality, or national honor, or the ethics of the marketplace? Can these things save us?

To believe in something is to trust in something, and what else can you trust and believe but the Savior, Jesus Christ: crucified, dead and buried, and on the third day raised up again?

And finally, if Jesus Christ was not raised from the tomb, all your living is in vain. You have nothing to live for, and nothing to hope for after you die. Paul says that if Christ was not raised, there is no resurrection for anyone. There is no eternal life, and thus, there is no meaning in this life. Everything that is, begins and ends with what you see here and now. Everything that matters is before your eyes. After that, there is nothing without the empty tomb.

"Lord, I believe; help Thou my unbelief." You can approach the question logically, and determine that the gospels must be telling it as it really happened. You can consider the cost of not believing, and conclude that if you are to find any meaning or hope in your life, you have no choice but to believe.

But in the end, it is a matter of faith. Logic can only *prepare* you to believe; faith *makes* you believe. It is something you cannot explain, because faith is finally a gift from God, but one day, you know it is true. One day, you know it in your bones, in your heart of hearts, and in the very depths of your soul: Jesus Christ was raised from the dead!

This makes all the difference. Everything we are, everything we hope for and live for, everything we believe depends on this. He has given us the victory we couldn't win for ourselves, and the power to live in the fullness of God's grace.

Now we all can come to the empty tomb and say, "I believe." Now we all can lift up our voices and say of our Risen Lord,

> *Because He lives, I can face tomorrow,*
> *Because He lives, all fear is gone.*
> *Because I know He holds the future.*
> *And life is worth the living just*
> *because He lives.*
>
> (Gloria, William Gaither)

Today we all may say, "Why seek the living among the dead? He is not here, He is Risen! Christ the Lord is Risen today! Alleluia! Glory to God in the Highest! My preaching is not in vain. My faith is not in vain. My living is not in vain, because Jesus Christ is raised up from the dead, to live and reign forevermore, worlds without end." Amen.

Pastoral Prayer

Most Holy and Blessed God, who makes our lives worth the living at the empty tomb, we pray today for knowledge of heart and conviction of spirit. We believe, O Lord; help us with our unbelief.

We believe we are made new in the Risen Christ; help us to live new lives now in Him.

We believe we have received the gift of everlasting life by Christ's victory over the grave; help us now to be filled with grace and confidence in the promises of all eternity.

We believe heaven and earth show Your glory today because death has lost its sting; help us to be glorified in all we think, and feel and do, that goodness and mercy shall follow us all the days of our lives.

Gracious, Most High and Holy God, who was, and is, and evermore shall be: hear our grateful prayers of praise today. We have come through the gathering clouds of Lent. We have sat in this place in utter darkness on the night our Lord was betrayed. Now we stand together in the bright light of a brand new day. He is Risen, and because He lives, all fear is gone. Hope sits on the throne and doubt is banished to the shadows. Because He lives, we now are ready to go forth into the world with the good news on our lips, and the secret of everlasting life planted in our hearts. We give our thanks today in the name of Jesus Christ, our Crucified and Risen Lord. Amen.

sunday after easter
Wounded Glory
Text: John 20:18-23

When He had said this, He showed them His hands and
His side. (John 20:20)

Have you ever wondered what Jesus really looked like?
The Bible is no help whatsoever in telling us, since it doesn't
say a thing about the physical appearance of Jesus. Not a sin-
gle word. We don't know if He was tall or short, skinny or
fat. We don't know if He had a straight nose, crooked teeth,
long hair or a beard. Everyone has a portrait of Jesus somewhere in their home, but no one knows what He looked like
in the flesh.

Have you ever wondered what Jesus looked like after He
was raised from the dead? I ask this as a separate question
because apparently, His appearance was changed after His
resurrection. In last week's text for Easter Sunday, we saw that
Mary didn't recognize Jesus in the garden, even though she
had surely known Him well for several years. And here in today's text, as Jesus appears to the disciples who are gathered
in a room together, again, for some reason, they don't recognize Him either.

They don't recognize Him, that is, until He shows them
the marks on His hands and in His side. The Man they knew
from Nazareth has returned to them exalted as the Risen Christ,
but they only recognize Him when He shows them His wounds
— the worldly signs of His sacrifice and suffering upon the
cross.

There is a profound spiritual lesson in this little episode
which is ours to learn today. The question is: how do we recognize Christ when He appears in our midst? How do we know
where Christ is, in our lives and in the world? Remember the

disciples on that first Easter day: they saw the Christ who was Risen in glory, but they recognized Him only when they saw His wounds.

I have seen this so often in my years of ministry that I would say it is almost always true: when troubles and tragedies hit in life, some people are helped by their faith while others lose their faith completely, and the difference almost always has to do with the way they see Christ.

There are many people who loudly and publicly profess their faith to anyone who will listen. They love Jesus so much, and they want you to know how much they love Jesus. They want to tell you how much Jesus has done for them and how much He can do for you. Judging by their talk, life can be just a continuous, uninterrupted joyride with Jesus if only you have the faith.

But then trouble or tragedy strike. They suffer a financial setback or a career disappointment. Something happens that isn't "supposed" to happen to people who love Jesus, like a divorce, or a child running away from home. Something happens that no amount of faith or prayer can change, like the death of a loved one.

Then, these are often the very people who lose their faith altogether. The whole structure of their religion comes tumbling down like a house of cards. The experience is shattering, and they cannot cope with their loss. Some people never recover the faith they were once so certain they had.

People like this lose their faith because it was built on a foundation of sand (Matthew 7:26). They built their whole faith on the idea of blessings and prosperity, so they were totally unprepared for the harder side of life. Their Jesus was clean and pure and far removed from the trials and troubles of this world; He was a kind of cosmic Santa Claus dispensing goodies to the people of His choosing. The problem is: this kind of Christ can't deal with their suffering! This kind of Christ has no answer for them when life is no longer prosperous or a blessing.

Meanwhile, other people are more quiet and humble about their faith. Maybe they don't witness as often as they should, but faith to them is a private matter. They are the "salt of the earth" type Christians whom Jesus described when He said, "Blessed are the meek," and "Blessed are the poor in spirit."

Yet these are often the very people who endure the tragedies of life with dignity and grace. Their quiet faith helps them through the valleys of pain and sorrow, and they know they never walk alone. You see, they have faith when they need it the most, because their Jesus isn't merely a supernatural sugar daddy who is helpless in the face of adversity. Their Jesus is the One who died on a cross and rose again — the One who comes to them in their trouble and shows them the wounds in His hands and side.

It is remarkable how healing and powerful it is to recognize Christ like this, to recognize Him by His wounds and not just by the blessings He bestows. It is remarkable how comforting it is to see that Christ is standing with us in our troubles.

I think of someone like Dr. Paul Brand, an American physician who worked with lepers in the town of Vellore, India. He worked in an isolated colony for people with this disease, who were shut off and quarantined from the outside world.

One day, the patients were holding a worship service as Dr. Brand came in late and sat in the back. But when they saw him, they insisted that he speak, and the doctor reluctantly agreed. He went up to the front and stood silently for moment.

He looked at all the patients assembled there, and he found himself looking at their hands. Many of them had the familiar "claw hands" which afflict people with leprosy. Some of them had no fingers; some just had twisted, deformed stumps where their hands once had been. Many of them sat on their hands or hid them from view, so ashamed were they of their appearance.

Dr. Brand began to speak. "I am a hand surgeon," he said, and waited for the translation into Tamil and Hindi. "So, when I first meet people, I can't help but look at their hands. I can tell what trade you were in by the position of your callouses and the condition of your nails. I can tell you something about your character. I love hands.''

He paused for a moment and said, "I've often wondered what it would have been like to meet Christ and study His hands. There were the hands of Christ the carpenter, rough and bruised from working with saw and hammer. There were the hands of Christ the healer, radiating sensitivity and compassion.''

"Then there were His crucified hands. It hurts me to think about the soldiers driving nails through His hands because I know what would happen to the nerves and tendons. His healing hands became crippled and gnarled, twisted shut on the cross.''

"Finally," the doctor continued, "there were His resurrected hands. You and I think of Paradise as a place of perfection, but when Jesus was raised up from the dead, He still had His earthly wounds and He showed them to His disciples.''

The effect on the audience of lepers was electric: "Christ had crippled, claw-like hands like mine? Christ showed His hands to His disciples when He was raised from the dead?'' Suddenly, this whole room full of lepers began pulling their hands out of their pockets and holding them up in the air. They knew Christ as one of them; they recognized Him in their midst, and He lifted them out of their shame.[1]

Let us not forget the social dimension of recognizing Christ, since we see His wounds not just in our own lives, but also in the life of the world. Where do you think Christ is, or where do you think we can recognize Him in the world today?

Can we recognize Him in our own hemisphere today, in neighboring nations like Brazil and Guatemala, Haiti and El Salvador? Can we see Him in the masses of peasants in those lands, who grow up in a poverty you and I can scarcely imagine? Half of their children die in infancy. They live in squalid mud huts and draw their water from filthy streams with garbage and raw sewage floating by.

In the cities, they beg and panhandle. In the country, they work on land which is owned by the wealthy few. Although they are hungry themselves, they watch good land being used to grow food for export to North America, because that is the system which is most profitable to the companies and the landowner.

If they complain or agitate for change, they are liable to be arrested in the middle of the night and perhaps tortured. If they fight for food, a fair share of the land or the right to form a union, they are liable to be killed by the death squads. It is a helpless, hopeless life they lead, with the power of the police, the wealthy elite and the North American colossus all lined up against them.

If you are wondering why there is so much anti-American sentiment in most parts of the Third World today, you must look at the bitter reality of imperialism. You must ask yourself why our national government and multinational corporations have so often lined up on the side of the wealthy few at the expense of the many who are poor.

Where can we recognize Christ in a world such as this? Can we recognize Him in the presidential palaces, plantations and corporate board rooms, far removed from the cries of the people? Or, do we recognize Christ in the swollen bellies and the hungry eyes of the little children, clinging to their mothers' skirts on the mud-soaked streets of peasant villages?

The answer lies in the experience of the disciples on that first Easter. They recognized the Risen Christ when they saw His wounds — the marks on His hands and the hole in His side.

● ● ●

Now that Christ is Risen from the grave, how will we recognize Him when we see Him? How will we know what He looks like, and where shall we find Him — in our own lives and in the life of the world?

He is our Risen Lord, exalted above all the earth, but He is not distant or detached from us. He is standing here beside us when life is neither kind nor fair. He shows us the marks on His hands and in His side, that our joy may be complete as we behold our Risen Lord in all His wounded glory. Amen.

Pastoral Prayer

Most Gracious and Loving Lord, we thank You for the bright light which has come into our world since Easter day. We thank You for the hope, the joy, the unquenchable faith which we have found at the empty tomb. Help us to celebrate this death of death by living as people redeemed in the Way, the Truth and the Life.

O God, who has met us in the flesh in Your Son, Jesus Christ, help us to recognize Him in our midst today, as the disciples did of old. Help us to see Him in the wounds we bear in life, and in the wounds which bleed our world. As we prepare to gather at His table today, inspire us to make our whole lives a sacrament, offering our bodies and our minds, our hearts and our spirits in service which is acceptable to You, even as He has been Servant to us. Through Jesus Christ we pray. Amen.

---

[1]This story is told in Philip Yancey's *Where Is God When It Hurts?*, (Zondervan Publishing House, Grand Rapids, MI, 1977), pp. 163-165.

children's lesson
Why The Holy Spirit?
Text: John 20:18-23

---

*He breathed on them and said, "Receive the Holy
Spirit."*   (John 20:22)

Suppose you had a hundred dollar bill in your hand, and
you announced that you wanted to give it away. You'd be pretty popular, wouldn't you! You'd probably get visited by every friend you ever had, and even some friends you didn't know
you had. They would all come by to see you once they heard
you had a hundred dollars to give away.

Now suppose a hundred friends of yours were gathered in
a large room, and you were there to give away your hundred
dollar bill. As you looked out at all their smiling faces, you'd
have a real problem on your hands. Who would get the money?
You've got a hundred people there, but only one bill to give
away! How would you decide who the lucky person would be?

Well, the best answer would be to go to a bank, and ex-
change your hundred dollar bill for 100 one dollar bills. That
way, you could spread the money around to everyone, and
no one would be left out.

That's a bit like what Jesus did when He gave His friends
a gift much more valuable than money: the gift of the Holy
Spirit. The Bible says that shortly after Easter, when Jesus was
raised from the dead, He visited His friends; and on one of
those visits He breathed on them and said, "Receive the Holy
Spirit."

Jesus was getting ready to go to heaven to live with God,
but He didn't want to leave His friends alone by themselves.
He wanted to leave a part of Himself, and a part of God, with
them. But how could He do that? Jesus Himself was just one
person, and He could only be with those people who were lucky

enough to be near Him. Only a few certain people would have the great privilege of being so close to God. What about everyone else? What about all the other people in the world who lived far away, and all the people like us, who were born many years after Jesus lived on earth?

Jesus Himself was like that hundred dollar bill — He could only be in one place at a time. But the Holy Spirit is like the 100 one dollar bills — God in the Holy Spirit can be everywhere at once. No one need be left out. The Holy Spirit is God's way of spreading Himself around and being a part of everyone. What does it mean to have the Holy Spirit? You'll find out more about that as you grow in faith. For now, let's just say that the Holy Spirit is Jesus' special gift to us after Easter. But at least you know now why He gave us this gift: it is His way of being with us all the time, and being with everyone who loves Him. Amen.

OLD TESTAMENT

Index Of Scripture Texts Used

NEW TESTAMENT